POWER
CRYSTALS

"An original and creative contribution to the world of crystals. DeSalvo reveals the magic and power behind quartz crystals and crystal skulls. His practical instructions for using crystals to communicate with angels are invaluable. I recommend this book as a down-to-earth guide to using the energy of the crystals to support the connection of the physical and spiritual worlds."

SUNNY DAWN JOHNSTON, AUTHOR OF
INVOKING THE ARCHANGELS

"This incredible book may well be DeSalvo's greatest work as he unravels the mystery behind the incredible power of quartz crystals as well as ancient crystal skulls. This book should not be missed!"

JOYCE KELLER, HOST OF THE *JOYCE KELLER SHOW*
AND AUTHOR OF *CALLING ALL ANGELS*

POWER
CRYSTALS

Spiritual and Magical Practices,
Crystal Skulls, and Alien Technology

JOHN DeSALVO, Ph.D.

Destiny Books
Rochester, Vermont • Toronto, Canada

Destiny Books
One Park Street
Rochester, Vermont 05767
www.DestinyBooks.com

Text stock is SFI certified

Destiny Books is a division of Inner Traditions International

Library of Congress Cataloging-in-Publication Data

DeSalvo, John A.
  Power crystals : spiritual and magical practices, crystal skulls, and alien technology / John DeSalvo.
      p. cm.
  Includes bibliographical references and index.
  ISBN 978-1-59477-400-3 (pbk.) — ISBN 978-1-59477-702-8 (e-book)
  1. Crystals—Psychic aspects. 2. Crystal skulls. I. Title.
  BF1442.C78D47 2012
  133'.2548—dc23

                                                              2012001414

Printed and bound in the United States by Lake Book Manufacturing
The text stock is SFI certified. The Sustainable Forestry Initiative® program promotes sustainable forest management.

10   9   8   7   6   5   4   3   2   1

Text design by Jack Nichols
Text layout by Virginia Scott Bowman
This book was typeset in Garamond Premier Pro and Gill Sans with Caslon Oldface and Gill Sans used as display typefaces

To send correspondence to the author of this book, mail a first-class letter to the author c/o Inner Traditions • Bear & Company, One Park Street, Rochester, VT 05767, and we will forward the communication, or contact the author directly at **drjohn@ gizapyramid.com** or **www.gizapyramid.com**.

To my supportive family:
My wife, Valerie, and my children, Christopher,
Stephen, Paul, and Veronica.

To my true sister and brother,
Joanne St. George and Paul Di Salvo.
May God bless them for all they have done
for me since childhood.

And most especially
to my parents, Nina and John DeSalvo,
who started all this by buying me my first quartz crystal
when I was just a small boy.

Contents

Foreword

JoAnn Parks

Metaphysical things were never part of my life, and I had never ever heard of crystal skulls. However, being the only child in my family, I have always tried to have an open mind and a willingness to learn. I believe if people do not have this attitude, they will lose their vision in life.

My crystal skull odyssey started in 1973 when my husband and I met a very famous healer by the name of Lama Norbu. He had been instructed in the healing arts of a Tibetan sect in India, and, when his training was complete, he left the sect and traveled to Guatemala, where he was given a crystal skull as a gift to use in his healing work. That skull is today known as Max. Eventually Lama Norbu wound up in Houston, Texas, which is where I met him. I would go on to work with him for many years.

At about the same time that we met Lama Norbu, our family medical doctor diagnosed our twelve-year-old daughter with a very rare form of bone cancer, and she was given three months to live. No words can describe how devastated we were. Soon thereafter we began to work to try and heal her, together with the Lama and his crystal skull. The doctors were subsequently amazed and baffled when we were able to extend our daughter's life for three additional years, which I attribute to the special healing work we did.

I ended up working for the lama for the next four and a half years, not really knowing why, but trusting that there was a reason for it. Many wonderful things went on at his shrine where we worked, things I can't explain. In hindsight I believe it was all part of a learning experience that I was supposed to have; I believe that this learning experience was preparing me for what was to come. In 1977, before Lama Norbu died, he gave my husband and me the crystal skull. He told us, "Take care of the skull, and one day you will know what it is for and about." Well, the only thing we knew at that point was that Lama Norbu and the other monks used the skull on their altar as a spiritual healing tool.

My husband, Carl, and I took the skull home and placed it in a box in a closet, where it remained for the next ten years. The skull was not silent during this time but spoke to me in dreams, telling me to find "the man." I thought I was going crazy! For the next decade I would hear this rock talk to me in my dreams and in my mind. One of the things the skull told me was that, he, the skull, was important to humankind and wanted to serve us in a very special way.

One day in 1987, I turned on the television set to *Good Morning Houston*. On the show, people from a UFO association in Arizona were being interviewed. As part of the interview they displayed two photographs, one of an Egyptian bust and the other of a crystal skull. I called the station and the staff helped me locate the people featured on the show. When I explained that I, too, had a crystal skull, the people from this UFO association offered to visit our home to see and assess it. When they arrived, I took the skull out of the box and showed it to them. At that point they said to me, "You have something very rare. Little is known about these skulls," and they suggested that I take it to the Houston Museum.

I went there the next day, and the people who looked at the crystal skull reiterated what the previous folks had said, and then offered to put it on display in their museum. I thanked them for their advice and offer but told them that because they didn't really know anything substantial about the skull, it didn't seem right to put it on display.

I brought the skull back home, placed it back in the closet in its box, patted it on the head, and said, "Well, skull, we will find 'the man' one of these days." Very loudly in my mind I heard the skull say, "By the way, my name is not skull, my name is Max." I jumped up and looked it in the eye and said, "Holy moly, I have a rock in a box and he has a name!" Shocked, I told the skull to "leave me alone," then I closed the box, threw some pillows over it, and pushed it a little farther back in the closet.

More, however, was in store for me. The skull talked to me again in my mind and told me to call the station back, which I really did not want to do but I did it anyway. The people at the television station put me in touch with someone who put me in touch with someone else: a man by the name of Mr. F. R. Nick Nocerino, who lived in California.

Nick Nocerino turned out to be the world's foremost authority on crystals and crystal skulls. He founded the Crystal Skull Society in 1945, which identified, documented, and researched crystal skulls worldwide. Nick was also a teacher and researcher and taught classes, in fifty-two countries, on how to heal with crystals and crystal skulls. In addition, he led more than thirty research groups in the United States. These groups were comprised of engineers, doctors, anthropologists, and computer scientists who were fascinated with crystals skulls and intent on learning more about them.

Nick owned an ancient crystal skull by the name of ShaNaRa, and he believed that these ancient crystal skulls were important for humanity. He was "the man" who Max had wanted me to find; apparently Nick had been looking for my particular crystal skull since 1949!

A lot of synchronistic things began to happen at that point. (At the time, I didn't even know what the word *synchronicity* meant, but I later reasoned that perhaps meaningful coincidences were God's secret way of arranging things!) I had no intention of sharing Max with the public, but people started calling me, wanting to see Max and to spend time meditating with him. Thus, I decided to travel with him all over the United States to do just that. As time went on, these trips became more frequent and Max's popularity grew and grew until he became one of the world's most famous ancient crystal skulls.

In 1996 a laboratory at the British Museum in London invited us to bring Max to their lab for testing. They were testing seven crystal skulls in total, including ShaNaRa and some other alleged ancient crystal skulls. We went to London to get an honest opinion from the lab researchers; however, after the research had been completed, they would not release any test results on Max or ShaNaRa, even though they had told us beforehand that we would be privy to the fruits of their research. Their rationale was that because these skulls were privately owned, they couldn't comment on them. We thought this was ridiculous! Why did they have us go to all the trouble to bring Max there in the first place? To me they said a lot by saying nothing. A documentary on the British Museum's research undertaking, titled *The Mystery of the Crystal Skulls,* was later produced in 2008 and aired every three months for a period of three years on A & E after its initial run in England.

Max has subsequently been examined by experts from all over the world, and they all conclude that he was not carved with modern-day tools. He was created or carved from a crystal with five different growth patterns instead of being carved from one solid piece of crystal. Photos of Max sometimes show radiant energy fields around him, which have the structure and resemblance of bone. At times he changes colors, appearing to have pupils that look right at you.

As a result of my travels with Max, I have seen numerous other crystal skulls—in all shapes, sizes, and colors—all of them allegedly ancient. Many of these have been from China, Mexico, and Brazil. I question the authenticity of many if not most of them because unless a crystal skull has been lab tested, one can't say with any certainty if it's ancient, old, or modern. Apart from the 1996 British Museum study and studies by John DeSalvo (which he will be discussing in this book), I know of no other formal scientific studies on any crystal skulls to date.

Yet, if a crystal skull does not turn out to be ancient, this shouldn't matter to its owner. What's important is what a person believes about the skull and how people interact with it. These skulls have had a positive impact on many people all over the world and have touched thousands of individuals. What's significant is that these skulls have become tools of service to others, in that they have healing powers that include not only physical healing but also spiritual, emotional, and mental healing.

I have been Max's keeper for thirty-five years and have shared him with the world for twenty-five. He has a very gentle and loving energy and loves to help people any way he can. He is not just a physical object but a living being full of energy and light. When people come up to Max and experience being with him, they may have one of many diverse reactions. They may cry, they may kiss Max on the head, they may fall into a deep meditation—one never knows quite what may happen, and there is no right or wrong experience. Each individual is, in interacting with the skull, honoring their own "self" and whatever emotions may arise in them when they come before him. Through Max we have the opportunity to look at ourselves and see the truth and our value and worth, or we have the choice to turn and walk away unaffected. It's all up to the individual. It is my personal hope that many people will continue to take the opportunity to meet Max and experience his spiritual energy and healing powers.

This new book on quartz crystals by my good friend John DeSalvo, with its emphasis on crystal skulls, is timely, significant, and necessary. There is much false and exaggerated information on the topic of crystals and crystal skulls, so it is great to have a definitive work by one of our more acclaimed researchers of unusual and often misunderstood phenomena. We wish you and your own personal crystal skull all the blessings in the world and hope you enjoy this wonderful and edifying book!

JoAnn Parks, a resident of Houston, Texas, is the current caretaker of the crystal skull known as Max, which many people consider to be one of the rarest artifacts found on Earth. Max is known nationally and internationally and has been featured in several documentaries worldwide. He communicated to JoAnn that he comes from both the Pleiades and Atlantis.

Acknowledgments

I would like to thank the following people for all their help and support in my writing of this book.

Judy and Marty Stuart, two gifted psychics who have been my very dear friends for many years, for their continual encouragement and generous help with all my books on spiritual matters. Judy read this entire manuscript and made many important suggestions.

Seann Xenja, owner of Dynamic Energy Crystals (www.dynamicenergycrystals.com) in Sausalito, California, who has generously supplied me with many wonderful color photos of rare and diversified crystals in his collection and from his store, and who was willing to take extra photos of special crystals for me.

Becky Andreasson, my very good friend and colleague for many years, who has contributed her personal experiences with alien implants to this book. I don't know what I would do without her constant friendship and support for all my research.

Helene Olsen (www.AngelsLighthouse.com), a highly gifted psychic medium, good friend, and research colleague, who has contributed much information to the chapter "Meditating with Crystals" from her personal experience and many years of teaching meditation. She also called my attention to my omission of Lemurian crystals, which I have remedied by including a section on this interesting and fascinating type of quartz crystal.

Bryan Bandli, manager of the SEM/EDS lab at the University of Minnesota, Duluth, for his expert SEM/EDS testing of the Himalayan crystal skull in my possession.

Scott Wolter, my very good friend and research colleague, who is president of American Petrographic Services in St. Paul, Minnesota. Scott is the world's leading researcher on the Kensington Rune Stone (the Hooked X), and he has been an invaluable expert for the testing of my artifacts and crystal skulls.

Linda Frisch has been such a supportive friend throughout this research and has supplied me with the wonderful photos of her Himalayan crystal skull and her Dropa disc. Linda's gifted insight with crystals and jade has helped me tremendously in my research, and I am grateful to her for the many hours of discussions we've had.

Kirby Seid, who was the caretaker of ShaNaRa, has been a wonderful friend and supporter of my research throughout the years. He has contributed wonderful photos to this book. Kirby is always willing to give me his advice and suggestions whenever I have a question. You can see his creations at www.lightlabyrinthproject.com and www.seidcrystals.com.

Nick Nocerino, who is considered the father of crystal skull research. Nick's work and research in this field will be appreciated for decades to come. Nick was my very good friend and an inspiration for my own crystal skull research. He died in 2004, and I miss him very much.

Khrys Nocerino has been a wonderful friend for many years. If she had not stored my ancient crystal skull in her sewing room for eight years, I probably would not have written this book. I am grateful to her for not discarding it or giving it away but patiently keeping it for me until such time that I would want it back. Thank you, Khrys, for your insight and friendship.

Michele Nocerino contributed wonderful photos of ShaNaRa, the Mitchell-Hedges crystal skull, the amethyst crystal skull, and the Mayan crystal skull, which I am most grateful for. I am very happy that Michele is continuing in her father's footsteps with ShaNaRa.

Warm thanks to Zane Grant for contributing the excellent photos of crystal skulls in his collection and also his help with my research in tracking down information about the plant resin that covers some of the Himalayan crystal skulls. Zane has also been very dedicated to advancing the knowledge of crystal skulls.

I also want to thank Terry Roses, one of the most interesting and brilliant people I have ever known. Terry contributed the photos of the crystal healing pouches of the Native American shamans, the Herkimer diamonds, and many other wonderful photos in this book.

Elizabeth HeartStar Keller has been a constant friend and supporter throughout my research. I am grateful for her friendship and the photos she has contributed to this book.

I am grateful to Kristin Reed and Nancy Bartell for also contributing photos of HeartStar, one of the small Himalayan ancient crystal skulls owned by Elizabeth HeartStar Keller.

Al Leone, one of my best friends and fellow researchers, who was my actual big brother during my Chi Phi fraternity days. Mama Leone, Al's mother, brought me to a real psychic for the first time in my life.

Jeanne Dunn, my very good friend and crystal skull colleague for many years, who discovered that my crystal skull was one of the eight ancient Himalayan crystal skulls. She also contributed photos to this book.

Carla Hansen has been a very good friend and supporter during my research. I thank her for all the information she has given me and her constant words of encouragement.

Becki Shields, for generously giving me one of her own personal and precious Lemurian crystals—for which I am extremely grateful—and for supplying me with information about Lemurian crystals

Dr. Frank Loo, my very good friend and colleague, who supplied me with the ancient Himalayan skull for my research. Frank is one of the most interesting people I have ever known and has been a constant supporter of my work. Also, I want to thank him for permission to use photographs of the Himalayan skulls.

Valerie DeSalvo, my wife and supporter of my research, who took the wonderful photos of the SEM/EDS lab, which documented all of our testing and research.

Ann Hall (www.AnnHallMedium.yolasite.com), a psychic medium and my good friend, for giving me her impressions of my ancient Himalayan skull.

Gary "Moonhawk" Butler, who had the insight and motivation to have the coating from one of the Himalayan skulls tested at the University of Utah several years ago. I would like to honor him for performing one of the first scientific and quantitative tests done on these crystal skulls. Gary was loved by many and died at an early age; he gave much comfort with his wisdom and healing skills. Lynn Johnson graciously supplied me with photos of her late husband, Gary, and information about his research, and I am very grateful to her for that.

The staff at Inner Traditions, who have had faith in my books and are dedicated to publishing the highest quality spiritual books for humanity. Jon Graham especially earns my gratitude for supporting me from the beginning and being a visionary individual. Anne Dillon, my editor, went beyond the call of duty in editing this book. This is my fourth book with Anne, and I am fortunate to have such a great editor.

JoAnn Parks, who graciously wrote the foreword to this book and has allowed me to spend time with Max. I have enjoyed our friendship immensely and am grateful for her constant encouragement and enthusiasm for my research.

The Fascinating World of Quartz

Good books on quartz crystals abound, so why do we need another one? My personal motivation to write and research this topic is fueled by a compulsion to make a unique contribution to the body of work that exists on a subject that intrigues me. Crystals have fascinated me since childhood. I believe that I can present quartz crystals in a way that is more revealing than what has been done to date.

The majority of the recent books on crystals have been authored by nonscientists, who tend to focus on New Age or psychic interpretations of crystals. In my opinion, the nonscientists who try to present a scientific viewpoint usually fall short. To write about any subject properly one must be objective and apply the scientific method whenever possible in order to separate truth from myth. Most of the currently available books on crystals solely promote the view of the author and do not objectively cover what may be other equally valid theories. As a former teacher and professor, I make it a practice to always present a plethora of viewpoints and evidence, even if it's conflicting, and allow students to make up their own minds. I do like to contribute my own personal research and opinions, but I am always clear that I am presenting my opinion and that I don't have all the answers either.

For many years I have been involved with research on many mysterious artifacts, including the Shroud of Turin, the alleged burial cloth of Christ. I am one of the few people that actually at one time had in my possession the sticky tape blood samples that were removed from the shroud during the 1978 studies in Turin, Italy. I was coordinating research with microscopy studies at that time.

I believed that some of the testing methods and procedures we used on the shroud could be used on ancient crystal skulls. I also felt that the research I had done on the Great Pyramid of Giza and pyramid research in general would be applicable to my studies of crystal and crystal skulls. In addition to my research into the shroud and pyramids, many years ago I was involved with researching what was allegedly Noah's Ark on Mt. Ararat. Colonel Jim Irvin, one of the astronauts who walked on the moon, was a collaborator of mine in this research. I still have a small piece of the wood that was recovered during one of the early Noah's Ark expeditions (the Navarro expedition in 1969).*

In addition to being a scientist, I have been a student of metaphysics and the paranormal since junior high school. I have always believed in the validity of paranormal events and the psychic world and have also believed that one could study them in an objective and scientific manner. Granted, even though, generally speaking, paranormal phenomena are not repeatable and thus the scientific method cannot always be applied, much of it can be objectively and clinically studied with scientific equipment and probability data. Because I have a foot in each world—the scientific and the paranormal—I believe I am in a good position to study quartz crystals and crystal skulls.

You will find a major section on ancient crystal skulls included in this book. Crystal skulls in general can be classified into three major groups based on when they were carved. This classification system is useful, although somewhat arbitrary. The first group is "modern" crystal skulls, which were carved within the past two hundred years, usually

---

*Ferdinand Navarro was a French industrialist who made four expeditions (1952, 1953, 1955, and 1969) up Mt. Ararat to look for Noah's Ark. In 1969 he found five pieces of wood on Mt. Ararat, which he attributed as wood from Noah's Ark. The longest piece was seventeen inches long.

by using modern tools and technology. The next classification is "old" crystal skulls, which were carved between two hundred and one thousand years ago. Finally, we have the "ancient" crystal skulls, the oldest ones being carved more than one thousand years ago. There are those who believe that some crystal skulls may be extremely ancient, possibly in the range of tens of thousands of years old.

This book primarily focuses on the ancient crystal skulls, not the old or modern ones. There are several reasons for this. The ancient crystal skulls are the most interesting because of their antiquity and the mystery surrounding their makers, when they were created, and their purpose. In reality we know of only less than half a dozen of these ancient crystal skulls. We will discuss what we currently know about each of them, including its current location, its provenance, its current ownership, what scientific studies have been carried out on it, and what, if any, interesting paranormal phenomena has been reported about it. (Of particular interest is the fact that these ancient skulls are the only ones that seem capable of producing paranormal or psychic activity.)

As a child I had an interest in both crystals and in human skulls. I recall that one of my favorite toys was a small plastic skull that when wound up would travel around a table with its teeth chattering, much to my delight. My parents always bought me one of these around Halloween when the stores carried them. I played with this toy so much that the wind-up spring usually broke within a couple of days and I had to wait for the next Halloween to get another one.

I have been a rock and mineral collector since the fourth grade. By the time I was in the sixth grade, I had a fairly large and impressive collection of rocks and minerals for a boy my age. I even had a microscope and ultraviolet light to study fluorescent rocks. I first exhibited my collection at my elementary school science fair, which was open to the public. A local newspaper reporter attending the fair thought my collection was so impressive that she took pictures of me with my collection, which graced the front page of our local newspaper the next day. My favorite rocks were petrified wood and, of course, interesting and unusual specimens of quartz crystals. They had a beauty and mystery beyond words, and I was mesmerized by something about them.

I was impressed with quartz for other reasons also. In high school I put together my first crystal radio using scrap electronic parts. I immediately picked up a local radio station, which came in very clearly. It was so amazing to me that a bunch of junk electronic parts and wires I had put together with solder and electrical tape produced such wonders! I knew the crystal (which was the receiver) was the key to all of this, and since that time I have been fascinated not only with the beauty and mystery of crystals but also with their properties.

Even while attending graduate school at the Johns Hopkins University, I was awed by the world of crystals. When we had the opportunity to experiment with an aspect of crystallography, I was struck by the incredibly intricate symmetry of the crystal lattice structures I was looking at and felt there must be some important purpose for this symmetry, maybe something not yet discovered. I kept all this in the back of my mind and hoped one day I could explore these ideas further.

My interest in the workings of the human body extended to my doctoral studies at the University of Illinois, where I taught human gross anatomy using dissected cadavers.* I was most interested in the anatomy of the skull and its composition. It's very interesting that after my first year of teaching college full time, my anatomy class presented me with an unusual gift in appreciation of my teaching. It was a life-size ceramic skull, which the entire class had signed and then glazed. I still have this today and treasure it.

Since college and graduate school I have continued to collect interesting crystal specimens. In my personal collection of artifacts I have a very rare and ancient cylinder seal from Mesopotamia, dating from roughly 4000 BCE. (Please see plate 1 of the color insert.) Its rarity can be attributed to its composition, which is quartz crystal. Most seals

---

*I was told by the head of the anatomy department, Dr. Stanley Stolpe, that I was one of the best dissectors he had ever taught. We eventually coauthored a book on human anatomy; it's titled *Human Anatomy—A Study Guide.*

from this period were made from stone, glass, or ceramics. Rarer ones were made from obsidian, hematite, or other elements such as lapis lazuli. They were fabricated by impressing an image into the seal, which when rolled onto wet clay, left the imprint of the pattern in the clay. Seals were used as personal identification to sign documents and other important cultural objects. I believe that my cylinder seal may have been used as a talisman because it has interesting line drawings on it, which I believe are magical signs.

It seems that quartz crystal is involved in many of the mysteries of the ancient world. I had been researching the Great Pyramid of Giza for more than a decade and this work revealed interesting observations about the use of quartz in ancient times. In 1986, two French architects, using electronic detectors, discovered a small chamber below the passageway that leads to the Queen's Chamber. They bored through a one-inch hole and found a cavity filled with crystalline silica (sand). The sand was analyzed and found to contain more than 99 percent quartz, which varied from 100 to 400 microns in size. This kind of sand is known as musical sand because it makes a whispering noise when it is blown or walked on. It appears that this sand may have come from El Tur in southern Sinai, which is several hundred miles from the Great Pyramid. Why would this type of sand be transported such a long distance and be placed in a sealed-off chamber in the Great Pyramid? What is the purpose of this quartz? This question and others that are equally intriguing continue to baffle scientists today.

Another interesting fact of the Great Pyramid is that the coffer in the king's chamber is composed of special, hard granite. Granite is composed of quartz, feldspar, and mica. One hundred blocks of granite make up the walls of the king's chamber. This chamber is noted for producing paranormal effects. People have had out-of-body experiences, seen visions, heard strange sounds, and experienced other kinds of strange phenomena here.

My personal fascination with crystal skulls arose approximately ten years ago, at which time I was put in touch with the world's foremost

Fig. I.1. The coffer in the King's Chamber of the Giza Pyramid, made from granite, which contains quartz, among other elements. Are the paranormal effects that have been noted here attributable to the presence of this quartz? Photograph courtesy of John Bodsworth.

expert on crystals and crystal skulls, Nick Nocerino. (Please see plate 2 of the color insert.) I had heard of Nick and his excellent reputation as an objective crystal skull researcher. In 1945 Nick was the founder of the first society of crystal skulls. In addition, he was one of the few people who could claim that he owned an authentic ancient crystal skull. Nick was also considered one of the first ghost hunters in the 1950s, and he had so many interesting stories that he even appeared as a guest on *The Tonight Show* starring Johnny Carson.

After hearing about Nick and his expertise with crystal skulls, I contacted him and we immediately became good friends. I think the fact that each of us was of Italian descent helped tremendously, because we shared a similar cultural upbringing. Nick and I were frequently in contact, and I looked at him as my mentor in this area.

Nick gave me many gifts and one of them was the large altar crystal featured in plate 3 of the color insert. Another gift he gave me was a modern crystal skull, about the size of a baseball, which he had bought about nine years prior. I treasure this crystal skull because it was one that he had used personally for many years. I named this skull Max Jr., because he looked similar to the famous ancient crystal skull Max, owned by JoAnn Parks. Nick told me that this crystal skull came from Madagascar, which mines excellent high-quality quartz crystal. (Please see plate 4 of the color insert for a photograph of Max Jr.)

At this time, as my interest in crystal skulls was developing, I contacted some of the owners or caretakers of known ancient crystal skulls and read just about every book published on the topic. I eventually was able to obtain an alleged ancient crystal skull of my own. It stayed in storage for many years because I became totally sidetracked by other endeavors that demanded all of my attention. I still hoped to eventually be able to conduct some research with it when I had the time. This book will tell the story about this ancient crystal skull and what I discovered about it.

The next important event in my crystal skull awakening was when the Indiana Jones movie *Indiana Jones and the Kingdom of the Crystal Skull* was released in 2008. The character of Indiana Jones was my hero, and I must have watched the other movies about him (*Raiders of the Lost Ark, The Last Crusade,* and *The Temple of Doom*) hundreds of times. This prompted me to start thinking again about getting involved in crystal skull research. Several years ago I decided to investigate any and all new books on crystal skulls that were on the market and found that most of them were not very scientific or analytical. They were filled with inaccuracies and seemed to accept every myth and story about crystals and crystal skulls without proffering any evidence to support their hypotheses.

That was actually a good sign. To further test the waters, I started a blog on my MySpace page about crystal skulls. The response was overwhelming. To this day I continue to get e-mails begging me to continue the blog. This is confirmation to me of the incredibly strong interest in crystals and crystal skulls among the public.

Thus it was that I undertook the writing of this book.

The combination of my diverse training and research experience in biophysics, human anatomy and physiology, neurophysiology, paranormal and psychic research, spiritualism, and magic make me an ideal candidate for researching and writing about crystals and crystal skulls. I am open to new and innovative ideas but also careful to not accept every idea presented to me without experimentation and a critical analysis of the data.

My hope is to be the first scientist/paranormal researcher to carry out the first objective study of ancient crystal skulls, which will not only present the old evidence in a new way but also bring new research to light. I hope you enjoy my efforts, as told in the pages of this book!

PART ONE

✴

All about Quartz

1
What Is Quartz Crystal?

Volumes of books have been written about the properties of quartz crystals (hereafter simply referred to as quartz). Topics include their physical characteristics; chemical structures; properties; use in science and technology; and metaphysical uses in healing, divination, and magic. What is the common denominator? What has been the reaction to quartz crystals since the first men and women walked on the Earth? I can sum it up in three sentences:

They are beautiful to behold (see).
They are soothing and tranquilizing to the touch (feel).
They are hypnotizing and mysterious to ponder (think).

Many people believe that we, as individuals, are made up of three components—the physical, the mental, and the spiritual. To adequately describe a human being, these three components must be examined. To explore only one or two would render an incomplete picture. All three essences of what it means to be human must be understood individually so that they can then be understood in the context of how they operate together.

This same approach should be used in the study of quartz crystal. (Please see plate 5 of the color insert for a photograph of a beautiful quartz crystal.) Thus, in order to fully glean its metaphysical properties we must first begin with the recognition of quartz as a physical substance with higher properties that depend on its structure and function. So let our journey begin.

A MOST ENIGMATIC SUBSTANCE

Although quartz possesses amazing physical and chemical characteristics, it is still an enigmatic substance that has been valued and held in awe by almost every ancient culture as a magical stone. The Earth is full of rocks and gems that are beautiful and tantalizing, but I believe there is something unknown, mystical, and magical about quartz that touches the spiritual, psychic, or intuitive part of our being and makes a connection to it. This is why we are drawn to quartz and find it the most mysterious and haunting of all the known elements. Is it so unusual that crystal balls have been one of the oldest forms of divination used by man? (Please see plate 6 of the color insert.) Is it hard to believe that magical amulets have been made out of crystal since early civilizations started making things? There is something very special about crystal that is unique and in order to adequately cover this subject, we need to first look at the physical and chemical properties of quartz.

When we refer to a quartz crystal we are actually using terms derived from two different languages. The term *quartz* is derived from a German word *quarz,* which is of Slavic origin, meaning "hard" or "cross vein ore." The term *crystal* is derived from the Greek *krustallos* and means something that is congealed by the process of freezing, such as ice, for example.

Quartz, which is composed of silicon and oxygen, is formed deep in the earth over millions and millions of years. It's a very common rock and comes in all shapes, sizes, and colors. The second-most abundant mineral on the planet, it is formed from high pressure and heat deep in the earth. As the quartz cools, quartz crystals are formed. Large holes are dug into the earth with high-powered equipment in areas where miners believe these quartz veins exist. This process is called surface mining.

Once a vein is found, the use of heavy equipment is halted and a gentler method is employed. At this point, miners typically work by hand with picks and shovels to reveal the vein more clearly. They must be careful not to ruin the quartz, so as a result, much patience and gentleness is used. The quartz is then removed and transported to a place where it is cleaned. Then it can be exported to other places to make into various objects.

In its natural symmetrical shape, quartz is hexagonal (six-sided) and is typically terminated at one end with six facets. This type of quartz is referred to as single-terminated quartz. (There is an exception to this—double-terminated quartz—which we will discuss later on.) Here are a few interesting facts about quartz crystal. After feldspar, it is the second-most abundant element in the Earth's crust. Its molecular configuration is SiO_2. In fact, the way the molecules of silicon dioxide bind together produces the different shapes of crystals. Quartz is therefore a silicon-based element and not carbon-based, as is life on Earth. Many different varieties of quartz exist, and we will discuss many of them. We will not, however, discuss lead crystal, which is not a naturally occurring quartz or synthetic quartz. Lead crystal is merely glass that has been infused with lead oxide; it does not form a crystalline structure.

When I tell someone I own an ancient crystal skull they usually ask me if I have tested it with carbon-14 dating. Carbon-14 dating has been used on other well-known ancient artifacts, including the Shroud of Turin, the Dead Sea Scrolls, and Egyptian mummy linen. I tell them that this would be nice, but the material tested has to be made out of carbon, that is, it must have the atom carbon as its basic building block. This is the case for artifacts like linen, which is made from plants, as well as ancient writing paper like papyrus and velum, and other material whose composition is carbon-based.

The structure of quartz crystal has silicon as its basic atom, not carbon. We currently don't have a dating test for silicon-based materials. Even if we did and we applied it to quartz crystal, it would only give us the date that the quartz was formed in a vein of the Earth, which would be millions of years ago, and *not* the date the crystal was carved, which is the date of importance to us. Thus, to try to determine the date of a crystal skull, we need to use other methods.

THE STRUCTURE OF QUARTZ CRYSTAL

We call quartz a crystal but what do we mean by crystal? It is a compound that has the property of forming organized, repetitive patterns of unique arrangements among its atoms and molecules. We are most familiar with this in solids, but it also occurs in liquids. Examples of liquid crystals include some cell membranes and certain solutions of soap. This crystal structure is sometimes referred to as a lattice, which is a symmetrically repeating pattern in the three-dimensional structure of the compound. In addition to giving the substance beauty, the crystal or lattice pattern allows the crystal to store vast amounts of information. The lattice structure is also responsible for many of its physical, optical, chemical, and electrical properties. We will see how this is so important in quartz crystals.

If you remember your high school chemistry, you were shown a large chart of symbols, which your teacher called the Periodic Table of the Elements. This table listed more than one hundred elements in a specific order. It started with an H and He at the top, which stood for hydrogen and helium, respectively, and then the next row had the elements Li (lithium) (reminiscent of the fictional dilithium crystals from *Star Trek* fame), Be (beryllium), and Bo (boron). Some elements that we may be more familiar with include C (carbon), N (nitrogen), O (oxygen), and F (fluorine).

The table is based on the atomic number of the atom, which is the number of protons in its nucleus. Number 1 is hydrogen; number 92 is uranium. These are the naturally occurring elements. Elements above

92 (93–112) are man-made. (Six more elements have been discovered [113–18]), but names have not yet been agreed on. Each atom can combine with another atom to form a molecule. For example, if you have one atom of oxygen, it can combine with two atoms of hydrogen to form H_2O, common water. If you have one atom of silicon, it can combine with two atoms of oxygen to form SiO_2, silicon dioxide, which is the basic molecule or building block of quartz crystals.

The molecules of SiO_2 can interact together and form a repetitive and symmetric three-dimensional structure called a crystal lattice structure. This is what gives quartz its unique and important properties. Many different molecules can form crystal lattice structures, but for the purposes of our discussion we will only address quartz.

Scientists can determine the makeup of a lattice structure by using a testing method known as crystallography, which determines the exact arrangement of the atoms in the matrix. The x-ray diffraction technique was one of the first to be developed and is still used today to determine the molecular arrangement of atoms in the crystal. It works by shooting a beam of x-rays through the crystal and recording how it bounces off. Through a detailed mathematical analysis, one can reconstruct the pattern that would produce this type of x-ray scattering and deduce the specific arrangement of the atoms.

PROPERTIES OF QUARTZ CRYSTAL

The hardness of minerals has been standardized using what is called a Mohs' scale. Compared to other minerals, quartz is relatively hard and strong. A diamond registers 10 on the Mohs' scale, whereas quartz sits at 7. Some examples of the hardness of other stones on the Mohs' scale are: talc = 1, calcite = 3, fluorite = 4, feldspar = 6, topaz = 8. To polish quartz, one would have to use a mineral that is equal or higher on the Mohs' scale, such as diamonds or diamond dust.

The piezoelectric effect is perhaps the most fascinating property of quartz crystals. When stress is placed across a crystal, it develops an electrical potential. When an alternating electrical potential is applied across the sides of a crystal, it will vibrate or oscillate at a specific frequency. The frequency depends on several factors, which include both the size and shape of the crystal. It can be shaped to oscillate at a specific frequency; in clocks this frequency is chosen to be 32,768 Hz. (Hz stands for hertz, which is the term for cycles per second.) This frequency can be counted using a digital counter and thus the frequency can be used to keep accurate time. Other crystals have this property, but quartz is especially suited to time-keeping applications because the frequency does not change as much with temperature fluctuations as it does with other crystals.

This piezoelectric property was discovered in 1880 by Pierre Curie, the husband of Madam (Marie) Curie. Because of this property, many applications for quartz have been developed in electronics, including the use of quartz crystals in radios and phonographs, and in precise timing instruments such as the quartz clock and computers. Quartz crystals have been harnessed in a variety of other ways in industry. They have been used as components of sandpaper, lenses and prisms, circuit boards, televisions, and radar. Quartz is even used to make cement. Quartz crystal also has the unique property of being able to transmit ultraviolet light, which glass cannot.

Perhaps quartz crystal was selected as the medium from which to carve crystal skulls because of its piezoelectric property and its use in information storage. Is it a storage device of unimaginable information? Can crystals interact or communicate in some way with a person's brain? (Maybe that's why they're shaped like a skull?) Can crystals interact with the subconscious mind and/or spiritual bodies? Can a person's mind transmit information directly to a crystal and have it stored for later retrieval by the same person or someone else, maybe someone from the future? Can quartz record information like a video recorder and then be played back centuries later? These are questions to consider.

Think about this. If quartz can record and store information from the past, then by unlocking this information, we can get a glimpse into our ancient past. (Please see Richard Shafsky's account in the appendix of his experiences with the Mayan crystal skull with regard to this.) Perhaps there are important messages that some ancient cultures wanted to pass on to us. Also, can people use crystals to see into the future? Perhaps there is a scientific basis for using crystal balls for fortune-telling. Do crystals cause some quantum effect that distorts space-time?

It's interesting that the Laser Physics Centre at the Australian National University in Canberra succeeded in "stopping light" in a quartz crystal for about one second, which holds out the promise that quartz crystal might possess the ability to store light information in the future.[1] So, if indeed the ancients used quartz because they wanted to store information in its structure, how would they do this without our technology (or did they have advanced technology?), and what type of information would they want to store? We will explore all of these questions later in this book.

TYPES OF QUARTZ CRYSTAL

When the term *quartz* is mentioned, most people envision a clear, colorless stone that resembles a six-sided prism terminated with a point at one end that is also six-sided. The reason that typically only one of the terminations of quartz has six sides and the other is flat or plain is because quartz is usually formed while it is attached to a base of some kind. The free side can form a hexagonal termination, and the other side remains flat because it is usually fixed to a rock. Of course, there are exceptions in that both terminations are hexagonal. We will discuss these later on.

Clear quartz is sometimes referred to as rock crystal. It differs from other types of quartz in that it can be transparent, meaning that it is clear, with light able to pass through it easily. Or it can be translucent, whereby light will pass through it but in a diffused manner. Translucent types of quartz include smoky quartz, milky quartz, rose quartz, pink quartz, amethyst, tiger's eye, and citrine. At the other end of the spectrum is opaque quartz, which light cannot pass through.

Some varieties of opaque quartz include agate, jasper, carnelian, and onyx. Sometimes these are very beautiful specimens, given their varied bands of patterns and colors, as anyone who has seen these samples can attest. Below is a brief description of the most interesting varieties of quartz.

Smoky quartz is usually grayish in color but also can be found in a dark gray-brown. (Please see plate 7 of the color insert.) Milky quartz is cloudy because liquid is trapped inside during the formation of the crystal.

Rose quartz varies in color from light or pale pink to a kind of reddish pink color. The elements of iron, manganese, and titanium found in this stone produce the coloration.

Pink quartz is the color of its name. The pink color is due to aluminum and phosphate. (Please see plates 8–10 of the color insert for photographs of rose quartz crystals.)

Amethyst is a purple color that varies from bright purple to a darker purple color. (Please see plate 11 of the color insert.)

Tiger's eye is a fibrous looking stone with gold to reddish brown coloring. Citrine has a variety of colors and shades from pale yellow to reddish orange to brown usually attributed to iron impurities. (Please see plate 12 of the color insert.)

Agate is a beautiful multicolored and banded stone with strong metaphysical properties. (Please see plates 13 and 14 of the color insert for examples of agate.)

Onyx also is multicolored and banded like agate, but its bands are straighter, whereas jasper is usually red to brown in color. Carnelian typically has a reddish orange color. Rutilated quartz is a very interesting stone as it contains inclusions or impurities of rutile* and looks

---

*Rutile is a mineral composed mainly of titanium dioxide (TiO_2). Its name is derived from the Latin *rutilus,* which means "red," and it does display a deep red color, especially when looked at with transmitted light.

like it has needles inside of it. (Please see plates 15 and 16 of the color insert.)

SPECIAL TYPES OF QUARTZ CRYSTALS

Herkimer Diamonds

I next would like to discuss a very interesting form of quartz that is popular in the New Age belief system. Terry Roses, my very good friend who specializes in gems and minerals, suggested that I include a description and photographs of a special type of quartz crystal known as Herkimer diamonds. Because of their exceptional beauty they are referred to as diamonds, but they are actually a form of quartz crystal. They are usually very small, although some varieties can be larger and were formed differently from most quartz.

Fig. 1.1. A collection of Herkimer diamonds.
Photograph courtesy of Terry Roses.

Herkimer diamonds are named after the location where they were first discovered: Little Falls in Herkimer County, New York. (Thus they are also referred to as Little Falls diamonds.) In the eighteenth century when workmen cut into dolomite stone in that area the crystals were found in the stone. (The Mohawks and other settlers already knew of the crystals' existence.) According to a book on mineralogy from the early 1900s, they were also found in other nearby counties and towns in New York, including Middleville, Salisbury, and Newport. Apparently this quartz was found in loose cavities in calciferous sandstone, or embedded in loose earth.[2] Herkimer diamonds have also been found in Arizona, Asia, the Middle East, and Ukraine. (Please see plate 17 of the color insert.)

Fig. 1.2. Smaller Herkimer diamonds. Photograph courtesy of Terry Roses.

Herkimer diamonds are different from most quartz crystals in that they are double-terminated and not single-terminated as common quartz is. Herkimer diamonds form slowly in solutions in dolomite cavities and are not anchored to any base; they float free instead. Thus, they have little contact with a rock chamber or dolomite host. Because of this they can form terminals at both ends. Double-terminated, or double-pointed, quartz crystals have six main sides, and each of their ends or termination points also have six sides, for a total of eighteen facets on each crystal.

Double-terminated crystals are known for their extreme clarity, and, in fact, many New Age advocates claim that they are very effective when used for healing and in meditation. I believe that one of the reasons for their popularity is because they are double-terminated and not single; psychic energy emanates from both ends of the crystal instead of just one. It's also possible that one end receives energy and the other transmits energy, and in this way the crystal acts as a laser, which gives it extra strength. This is my hypothesis and not

Fig. 1.3. Double-terminated quartz crystals.
Photograph courtesy of Terry Roses.

yet proven, and because we cannot prove this, I would suggest that if you are interested in these double-terminated crystals obtain some and experiment.

Native American shamans used double-terminated crystals in ritual healing. They are usually carried in specially made leather or cloth pouches and are considered to be very sacred. (Please see plate 18 of the color insert.) Some Native Americans use very small Herkimer diamonds in their sacred rattles, which are part of ritual healing ceremonies.

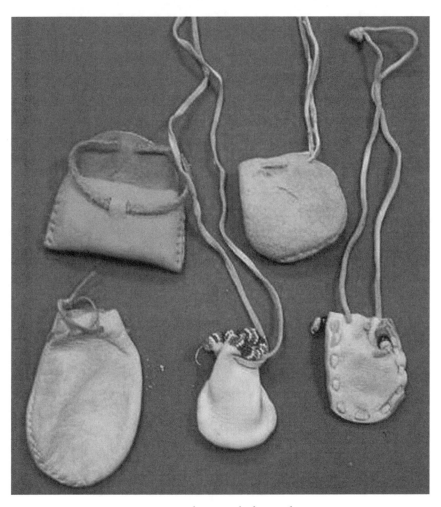

Fig. 1.4. Plain rawhide pouches.
Photograph courtesy of Terry Roses.

*Fig. 1.5. Medicine bag from the Black Elk family, with crest.
Photograph courtesy of Terry Roses.*

A Native American tradition refers to all quartz crystals, regardless of type, as grandmothers' tears, and the different colors of quartz represent the colors of life.[3]

Lemurian Crystals

What I enjoy so much about researching crystals is that it never ends and you never know what will come up next. This happened to me with a certain type of crystal that I had completely ignored. My good friend Helene Olsen, who is featured in the chapter on meditation and

Fig. 1.6. Rawhide pouch used to carry Herkimer diamonds.
Photograph courtesy of Terry Roses.

involved with my psychometry research, asked me how extensively I would cover Lemurian crystals in my book. I didn't know very much about them, only that some people claimed that they came from the legendary continent of Lemuria and that they had encoded information in them. This had sounded far-fetched to me and was probably the reason I stayed away from them.

I told her that I had not included anything about this type of crystal in my book but maybe I should look in to it as I wanted to be as inclusive as possible. As I started to research this specific and rare type of quartz crystal, I have to say that they started to pique my attention. The first thing I wanted to do was to obtain a specimen of one because I didn't have any in my collection.

Helene told me that she had recently been speaking with a woman by the name of Becki Shields who had a collection of Lemurian crystals, some of which she was planning to send to Helene. I immediately asked if I could have one. Helene mentioned this to Becki, who then told Helene that she had been planning to send me one anyway because apparently several days earlier she had been walking by her collection of crystals and one of the Lemurian crystals had called out to her and said, "Send me to John DeSalvo." (I had never met Becki, but she had been interested in my research and had listened to some of my interviews on the radio.)

This was very intriguing, because Helene had never mentioned anything to Becki about my interest in Lemurian crystals, nor had she even mentioned my name. This specific crystal that called out to Becki was an excellent specimen and a treasure that Becki had obtained many years ago. She loved all her crystals, but especially this one. It must have been difficult for her to give this one away because of her attachment to it. Because of this and other inexplicable things that have happened to me over the years, I have come to believe that a higher power does influence our work. The other interesting aspect of this was its timing. My book was undergoing final edits and additions, and all of this occurred about one week before I was scheduled to send in the final additions to it.

I remember reading somewhere that Lemurian crystals have a life of their own and do select who they want to be with. If you are the lucky person that a specific crystal wants to come to, you have a responsibility and an obligation to work with it and use it in a respectful and honorable manner, for your good and the good of others.

So, what are Lemurian crystals? Let's start with what geologists know about them and then cover their claimed metaphysical properties and my experience of meditating with them. It seems that attention was initially drawn to these types of quartz crystals when some were discovered by miners in the 1990s on a hilltop in the Minas Gerais region of Brazil. They were not discovered in clusters, like other quartz crystals, but found separately, buried in beds of sand. (They appeared almost planted like seeds. They are sometimes referred to as

Fig. 1.7. Lemurian crystal, also known as etched quartz crystal.
Photograph © John DeSalvo.

Lemurian seed crystals.) They have also been discovered at other sites, including a crystal cave in Arkansas, in the Ural Mountains of Russia, in Madagascar, and in a few other places.

What's so unique about them is that inscribed rows of horizontal, etched, parallel lines are found on one or more of their surfaces (another name for them is etched crystals).

I have studied them under a stereoscopic microscope and the lines look to be drawn with much precision. They are so precise and parallel it seems almost impossible that they would occur this way naturally. I remember a geologist who was studying alleged ancient rock formations in the ocean, and he said that sharp lines and borders that are seen in some geologic formations are almost always man-made. Some of the Lemurian crystals appear to have a matte finish and also give off a slight pinkish glow. These characteristics make them different from other quartz crystals, but they are quartz- and silicon-based and thus are definitely a form of quartz crystal. Why are they called Lemurian crystals? Lemuria is a legendary continent, like Atlantis, but it supposedly existed in the Pacific Ocean, not the Atlantic. Legends about Atlantis are very similar to legends about Lemuria. For example, they both had advanced technology and the people of both cultures were very psychic and spiritually developed. They could move things with levitation and had powerful weapons derived from crystal technology. Legend has it that Lemuria sank into the ocean just as Atlantis did and that the Lemurian crystals were placed or planted in Brazil and other areas of the world by Lemurians eons ago.

Supposedly, these lines or striations on their surface contained information about the Lemurian culture as well as other spiritual information including the Akashic Records, which is the record of all human thought and actions since the beginning of time. Rudolf Steiner, H. P. Blavatsky, Alice Bailey, and other well-known mystics and psychics have claimed that Lemuria did exist and the people there had special psychic powers. Rudolf Steiner claimed that Lemuria existed prior to Atlantis and its inhabitants were taught how to control nature by mental telepathy. Their culture surpassed ours in technology, the sciences, and the arts. They also could communicate with higher intelligences or gods.

According to Steiner, our planet had a very different environment at that time.[4] The air was more dense and the water less dense. There was much volcanic activity; fire emerged from deep within the earth. The so-called initiates in Lemuria had secret or spiritual knowledge, which they imparted to other worthy individuals. If Lemurian crystals were created, or at least carved, with these striations from this ancient advanced culture, it is exciting to think that they may contain information from this lost civilization. And if this code could be read or deciphered, what information and knowledge would it unlock?

Some people use Lemurian crystals for healing, some for opening up contact with spiritual beings or guides, some to try to connect with the ancient Lemurian culture, and others simply to enjoy their unique spiritual energy. It seems we are just beginning to unlock the potential uses of these crystals, both physically and psychically.

My meditation experience with them has made me believe that they are very powerful and they contain some type of unknown energy. They exhibit a warmth and vibration that I haven't experienced with other types of crystals or minerals. I can't say if it is a supernatural or a physical effect, but it's quite different from anything I have experienced before. This sensation or feeling is difficult to articulate in words; perhaps for each individual, the experience is different. Unfortunately, there are all sorts of claims but very little valid proof of anything, and until someone can unlock the mystery or code of these strange horizontal striations, we can only speculate about them.

I believe this is an important area for further research, but unfortunately the traditional or academic geologist probably will not pursue it because most of them don't take this theory of the crystals' origin seriously. They believe the cause of the etched lines and other markings are the result of unique pressure and temperature changes when the crystal was formed. I keep an open mind and believe they should be studied, both scientifically and psychically, to arrive at the truth. I for one will continue to research and experiment with Lemurian crystals and suggest you do the same.

Some people believe that Lemurian crystals open a channel to the dark side or evil entities and thus one should stay away from using them as a psychic tool. I think this is something to consider, because when any psychic tool is employed, channels that may connect to good or evil forces can be opened. It's my belief that all kinds of forces and entities are out there, and they want to talk to us. Thus, we must be careful and selective with whom we choose to communicate. That's why even with the use of crystals, I always recommend some type of protection before you begin working with them.

Later in the book I outline various protection techniques that you can employ. Use one that you are comfortable with, and hopefully this will help you filter out any negative forces and allow only the positive ones in. But again, this is uncharted territory, and you must use your judgment and decide what is right for you.

Synthetic Crystals

Synthetic crystals are produced in a lab. They are preferred over natural quartz crystals for technological applications because they can be made so as to have almost no flaws, as opposed to natural crystals, which are usually flawed. Also, synthetic crystals can be produced over weeks or months, depending on the desired size of the crystal, versus the eons of time necessary to form natural crystals. The synthetic crystal specimens can be made to order in the lab through a fairly simple process. High pressure and temperature are applied to silica grains, and electrical conduction is applied to cause crystal formation and growth.

A debate exists about whether synthetically produced quartz crystals have the same metaphysical properties as naturally formed crystals. I believe that most people involved in the metaphysical and psychic use of crystals believe they are not the same. These individuals feel there are little or no psychic, spiritual, or energetic benefits from synthetic crystals, believing they lack the energy or aura of natural crystals. This frequently prevents synthetic crystals from being used in meditation, healing, and energy work. Can there be something special about the crystals forming in the depths of the earth over millions of years that differentiates them from synthetic crystals grown in the lab in a short period of time? I will let the reader decide.

2
The History of Quartz

It seems we have a perception that our current civilization is the most advanced the world has known and that we currently are at the pinnacle of knowledge, wisdom, and technology. We believe that ancient civilizations were primitive and barbaric in their understanding of the world and the universe. But maybe this is an erroneous concept and it's actually the other way around. Maybe the ancients were far more advanced in knowledge and spiritual wisdom than we are today and *we* do not even come close to *them*.

If so, what could have happened to this wisdom and spiritual knowledge? Maybe it was lost through the ages and not passed down to us. Another possibility is that it was passed down to select individuals or groups and has been kept secret from the masses. Either way, we should be humble when we study ancient civilizations and not assume they were primitive and less advanced than us but look for hidden clues to determine whether they may have had some esoteric and secret wisdom that we do not. Thus we may learn and rediscover some esoteric teachings and wisdom that may be related in some way to our understanding of magical and spiritual gems, such as quartz crystals. Let's keep an open mind as we survey the ancient civilizations and probe their thoughts and understanding of this special mineral.

My guess is that one of the first metaphysical uses of crystals was for divination. I believe one of the earliest events may have been when early man, who had psychic ability, first picked up a crystal, looked into it, and accurately glimpsed the future. This definitely caught his attention. Maybe the prediction was for the hunt the next day and he saw what they were going to catch in the crystal. Or he saw someone's death, or some climactic event. Did all men and women at this time have psychic ability or only a few gifted individuals? We may never know, but I believe that primitive man had more or greater psychic ability than we have today. They had a simpler lifestyle, and because they were not constantly bombarded by television, radio, or cell phones, they lived close to nature and the Earth and were more in tune with the vibrations of the Earth and the spiritual realms. I also wonder if the fact that they slept close to the ground every night was a factor in stimulating or opening their psychic abilities.

THE SCHUMANN RESONANCE

I need to digress a little here and tell you about something very interesting that may be related to quartz crystals and their metaphysical properties. It appears that Earth gives off a certain frequency or resonance that can be measured by scientists; it is calculated to be 7.83 cycles per second. It is called the Schumann Resonance. It was discovered in 1952 by a German scientist named Winfried Otto Schumann, and it has been measured and confirmed by scientists around the world. It varies slightly in different parts of the globe, but the value of 7.83 is a good average and what most researchers and scientists use. Notice it is close to the alpha brain wave frequencies of 8 to 12 cycles per second. Some people claim to be able to actually hear it while others claim that humans and, in fact, all of life depends on this Schumann frequency or resonance and without it, we would not be able to survive. I think several other planets in our solar system may have their own Schumann Resonance, each unique.[1]

I was told that when NASA started manned space flights, especially long voyages to the moon, psychological and physical problems would crop up for some of the astronauts. It was suggested to place a Schumann resonator, which generated the frequency of 7.83 cycles per second, on the spacecraft. (It seems we cannot leave Earth for any length of time. My wife has always believed this and, in fact, often says that we were not meant to leave Earth. Maybe she is right.) Others have refuted this story and said NASA never used a Schumann resonator on any spacecraft or shuttle. We don't know if NASA actually did this and is denying it or they never did it. At this point, because there is no evidence to prove it, I personally doubt the story.

In any event, we are plugged in or tuned in to the Earth and maybe that is the secret of the paranormal phenomenon with crystals, because they are formed and grow deep within the earth, close to this Schumann frequency. Maybe the Schumann frequency generates a piezoelectric effect by its slight, wavelike pressurized effects. This is my hypothesis, and while I have no facts to prove it, I believe it's an important area of research to pursue, which I very much hope to be able to do in the future.

THE USE OF CRYSTAL BY ANCIENT CULTURES

One of the oldest documented uses of crystals in prehistoric times comes from China. In the small village of Zhoukoudian, about fifty kilometers from Beijing, fossils were discovered in 1918 by a Swedish archaeologist.[2] These later turned out to be fossils from Peking Man, or *Homo erectus,* who lived about a million and a half years ago.[3] Also discovered were many animal bones and stones of flint and limestone, as well as quartz crystals. It is believed that the quartz crystals may have been used as primitive tools or possibly even used for religious purposes.

Three years later, in 1921, paleontologists made another discovery at this location. They found more fossils and excavated more of the site and, in so doing, found quartz fragments, which archaeologists believe to have been primitive tools used by Peking Man.[4] They found other tools made of other types of stone, but quartz tools were by far the most prevalent. Primitive man obviously recognized that the hardness of this material made it a good choice for tool-making. Did they also recognize its metaphysical applications?

We know that the ancient Egyptians of 3000 BCE mined crystal and used it to make amulets and jewelry, among other things. Some amulets such as scarabs and other religious icons found wrapped in mummies are made of quartz crystal. The Mesopotamian civilizations also used quartz, and we see this in the form of ancient beads, jewelry, and cylinder seals unearthed in this part of the world. The ancients held this material in very high regard and used it for special religious and cultural objects.

Quartz crystals have been found in prehistoric North American sites also, including a burial site of the Yuma Indians, who lived in present-day California. This burial site dates to approximately 6000 BCE.[5] I believe these quartz crystals were used in the spiritual rituals of these Native Americans.

In April of 2002 in Chihuahua, Mexico, a unique discovery was made. Miners were drilling a new tunnel looking for silver and zinc. They discovered something spectacular in a cavern they drilled through. The temperature and humidity in the cave were extremely high and very dangerous for humans to be exposed to. The upper limit of time that one could spend in this cave was only fifteen minutes.

What the miners found in the cave staggered their imagination. They felt they were looking at a giant geode. What they saw were crystals as large as telephone poles and an incredible complex of all types of crystal formations. These large crystals were faceted, and some of them were as long as thirty-six feet and weighed as much as fifty-five tons. They were composed of selenite, a crystalline form of gypsum. Two chambers were found with these gigantic crystals, the larger chamber being approximately as large as a cathedral.[6]

What this tells us is that there are mysteries in the earth that we cannot even dream of! The discovery was featured on the National Geographic Channel and made international news. What is sad about all of this is that pumps have been keeping the water out of the cave, but there is some discussion that this is too expensive to be able to continue to do. If the pumps are turned off, the caves will flood and probably be destroyed. Let's hope someone intervenes to preserve this new wonder of the modern world.

Small quartz crystals have also been found on mummies in prehistoric Peru. They were obviously placed there for a religious or spiritual reason similar to the placing of amulets on Egyptian mummies. I own a small crystal scarab that was most likely found on a mummy.

Quartz crystal primitive tools have been discovered in Austria. These tools date back at least to 10,000 BCE. In France, spear tips made of quartz crystal have been found dating back to approximately 7,000 BCE. There are also stories that Merlin the magician had access to a crystal cave, and he wielded his power from the energy of the crystals. There are legends of the Druids also using crystals in their rituals, but again most of this is speculative.

Regarding the ancient Greeks and Romans, we know they used crystals for divination and healing. In certain parts of Greece, drinking glasses and jugs were made of rock crystal because the Greeks believed that this would give them good health and maybe even prolong life.[7] Sometimes a vision in the crystal accurately predicted when someone would die, either naturally or by accident. Not everyone was a seer, and many times they were young boys or girls who would live in special temples, which people could visit to ask their questions. It was important to select girls who had special psychic ability or a natural ability to be trained in this art.[8]

The Oracle of Delphi is one example of a gifted seer whom people would visit and ask questions. Each seer applied crystals and mirrors differently, depending on what method they preferred. Some practiced in a traditional way by looking into the crystal or crystal ball to see visions. Or they looked into a crystal or a mirror over a well; the reflection of these objects in the water would give the seer the answers they sought. Other practices were quite unique.

CRYSTALS IN ANTIQUITY

In ancient Rome, naturalist and philosopher Galius Plinius Secundu, popularly known as Pliny the Elder, had an interesting idea of where quartz came from. He believed it was water that was frozen over long periods of time. His evidence was that quartz was found near glaciers but nowhere near volcanic mountains (as mentioned earlier, the Greek word for "ice" is *krustallos*). He also discovered that quartz crystal could split light into the color spectrum.[9]

A more prevalent thought at that time was that quartz was formed when water descended from the heavens to the Earth. In so doing, it became solidified and formed crystals. Another version was that it was transformed into crystals, with the help of angels, as it fell from heaven.

Let's now turn to an ancient source familiar to most of us, which is the Bible. A significant reference to crystal is found in the Old Testament book of Ezekiel 1:22–28.*

Over the heads of the living creatures there was the likeness of an expanse, shining like awe-inspiring crystal, spread out above their heads. And under the expanse their wings were stretched out straight, one toward another. And each creature had two wings covering its body. And when they went, I heard the sound of their wings like the sound of many waters, like the sound of the Almighty, a sound of tumult like the sound of an army. When they stood still, they let down their wings. And there came a voice from above the expanse over their heads. When they stood still, they let down their wings.

And above the expanse over their heads there was the likeness of a throne, in appearance like sapphire; and seated above the likeness

---

*Unless otherwise indicated, scripture quotations are from *The Holy Bible,* English Standard Version (ESV), copyright 2001 by Crossway Bibles, a publishing ministry of Good News Publishers, used with permission. All rights reserved.

of a throne was a likeness with a human appearance. And upward from what had the appearance of his waist I saw as it were gleaming metal, like the appearance of fire enclosed all around. And downward from what had the appearance of his waist I saw as it were the appearance of fire, and there was brightness around him. Like the appearance of the bow that is in the cloud on the day of rain, so was the appearance of the brightness all around.

Such was the appearance of the likeness of the glory of the Lord. And when I saw it, I fell on my face, and I heard the voice of one speaking.

The Israelites believed that God's throne rested on a sea of beautiful, sparkling, pure white crystal. This is seen in Ezekiel: over the heads of the creatures there was a sea of crystal, upon which the throne rested. Thus crystal was an important part of the theophany, or, in other words, the appearances of God in the Old and New Testaments.

The next set of scriptures is from the New Testament in the book of Revelation, chapter 4, verse 6: ". . . and before the throne there was as it were a sea of glass, like crystal. And around the throne, on each side of the throne, are four living creatures, full of eyes in front and behind."

The next reference is also in Revelation 22:1 and refers to the river of life, which was bright as crystal. "Then the angel showed me the river of the water of life, bright as crystal, flowing from the throne of God and of the Lamb."

Again, the holy significance of crystal is emphasized. This passage implies that it contains the presence of God and his spirit. Finally, we have a reference to the New Jerusalem coming down from heaven and being as clear as crystal. "And he carried me away in the Spirit to a great, high mountain, and showed me the holy city Jerusalem coming down out of heaven from God, having the glory of God, its radiance like a most rare jewel, like a jasper, clear as crystal" (Revelation 21:9–11).

Many times in the Bible crystal is associated with God's presence and his attributes, rendering it very symbolic and spiritual. Crystal is also referenced in the writings of many of the mystical saints, including Saint Theresa of Avila* in her book *The Interior Castle.* It is interesting that the symbolism of water in dreams and visions of mystics are associated with the presence of God, the Holy Spirit, and even Jesus.[10]

EVIDENCE OF SCRYING IN ANCIENT CULTURES

Genesis chapters 37 and 39 tell the story of Joseph and how he was sold into slavery to the Egyptians. His brothers were jealous of him, because their father liked him the best and treated him better than his other sons. After Joseph was sold into slavery in Egypt, he rose to power there and was the second highest in command. (Only the Pharaoh was above him.) Years later, when there was a famine in Egypt, his brothers were sent there by their father to buy grain, and they appeared before Joseph. He didn't reveal his identity to them but gave them grain to take home. In so doing Joseph gave the following orders to his steward: "Fill the men's sacks with food, as much as they can carry, and put each man's money in the mouth of his sack, and put my cup, the silver cup, in the mouth of the sack of the youngest, with his money for the grain" (Genesis 44:1–2).

Joseph is playing games with his brothers when he orders his steward, after they have left, to go after them and inspect their sacks. The steward is then instructed to accuse the brothers of stealing Joseph's special cup. They had gone only a short distance from the city when Joseph said to his steward: "Up, follow after the men, and when you overtake them, say to them, 'Why have you repaid evil for good? Is

---

*Saint Teresa of Avila, also called Saint Teresa of Jesus, lived from 1515 to 1582 in Spain. A Carmelite nun, mystic, and later a Roman Catholic saint, she is a reformer of the Carmelite Order and widely considered to be, along with John of the Cross, a founder of the Discalced Carmelites. (I was a Third Order Carmelite for about eight years many years ago and taught Carmelite spirituality.)

it not from this that my lord drinks, and by this that he practices divination? You have done evil in doing this'" (Genesis 44:4–5).

Here we have one of the most famous patriarchs of the Bible owning and using a divination cup! I am convinced that this cup was used for scrying, and what better material than crystal can one use for scrying? Even though the biblical verse says it's silver, we do not know if this is correct, as Bible verses have been edited throughout time. Is it possible the cup was covered or decorated with sliver and the inside was made out of crystal?

The Hebrew word for "silver" could refer to white or a pale color (like in Greek) in certain contexts. If crystal was equivalent to the material that God's throne was on—and there are many references to crystal in ancient religious literature relating to God—this would be the most important material to use for divination. To me this is obvious. Of course, some may argue that it was also filled with a liquid, and thus the scrying was done by studying the liquid. However, remember that in Egypt crystal was valuable and sacred, and a divination cup for the second in command of the country would most likely have it made from the most valuable and sacred material, in other words, quartz crystal.

An interesting historical note is that during the times of early Christianity, around the fourth to the seventh centuries, many believed witches or evil spirits could be seen in crystals or mirrors. These spirits could tell of future events and give information to the person looking into these objects. Others claimed to be able to see evil spirits on the surface of water. These practices were all forbidden by the church, and the continued practice of them could lead to excommunication or worst.

Roger Bacon, who lived in the thirteenth century, was a Rosicrucian who, it was said, dabbled in the occult by practicing with crystals and other objects.[11] In medieval Europe crystal gazing was a well-known and popular method of divination and was used to contact good spirits and angels.

The crown jewels of Scotland, dating from the sixteenth century, are comprised of the crown, the scepter, and the sword of state. I have recently discovered that the scepter has a two-inch diameter crystal globe mounted on its top, in addition to other jewels. The Scottish believed that these stones were magical; their use can be traced as far back as the time of the Druids. The Scottish sometimes referred to these as "stones of power."

A very interesting belief stems from medieval times: In order to access visions by way of a crystal, one had to induce a spirit to enter and possess it. Thus the magician performed certain magical rituals and spells to force a spirit into his crystal and produce visions for him. Some believed the spirits were good, and others believed that they were evil.

LATER HISTORICAL REFERENCES TO CRYSTALS

In the sixteenth century, Dr. John Dee and his scryer, Edward Kelley, used crystal balls to contact angels. I have previously published two books on this specific topic. The Enochian magical meditation that I will be discussing and teaching you in a future chapter was obtained by this angelic contact.

The famous German mathematician and astronomer Johannes Kepler (1571–1630) wrote about the similarity of snowflakes and crystals: they both had hexagonal or six-sided shapes. Because of their similarity, he believed crystals were originally formed from liquids. Kepler also had the idea that crystals were a kind of reflection or image of the soul of the Earth.[12] This idea that crystals were formed from water or ice was prevalent in Europe until about the seventeenth or eighteenth century when French chemist and physicist Etienne-Francois Geoffroy, best known for his affinity tables, refuted the idea that crystals were frozen liquid and stated they were mere stones.[13] Thus we move more into a scientific and analytical approach to crystals in the seventeenth and eighteenth centuries. Many scientists at that time began studying crystals with the improved microscope, and many articles on the structure and effects of crystals were published.

Rene Just Hauy (1743–1822), a French mineralogist and Roman Catholic priest, discovered the geometrical law of crystallization. As a result, he is considered the father of modern crystallography. He determined that crystals are composed of basic units, which have the same form, but the way they are joined together produces different structures.[14] Not all studies on crystals were strictly scientific at this time. One example was a German clairvoyant and psychic, known as the Seeress of Prevorst, who lived in Germany in the early nineteenth century. Her life was documented by a Dr. Kerner, and through him we learn that she used all kinds of stones and gems, including crystals, to heal and as magical remedies. Each stone had a particular property and produced a specific physical and spiritual response, depending on the gem or stone.

I wrote a book about her and her spiritual experiences. It is titled *The Seeress of Prevorst*.[15] She is also mentioned in the writings about her life by Ennemoser, who states that sensitive psychics are usually stimulated or excited by certain minerals, especially ruby. He goes on to say that they are calmed when looking at quartz crystal. The greatest response from the seeress to gems and minerals was not derived by looking at them but by holding them or placing them on her body, especially the pit of her stomach. If she was in a deep trance state, the placing of crystals on her stomach awakened her from this state. If the crystal remained on her stomach for some time, she would go into a cataleptic state. We do not know why this occurred, but this is an example of one of many varied effects crystals can have on a clairvoyant.

Many people today who use crystals often obtain psychic feelings or impressions when they are held in their hands or placed on their body (chakras), rendering physical contact very important in crystal use. In my experience more people have results if they hold the crystal in their hand instead of putting it on a stand or a table to look into. This is consistent with what we talked about in the first chapter, the piezoelectric property of crystals. The resonance of the crystal, both physical and spiritual, tends to stimulate or enhance the psychic connection between the crystal and the holder.

In our last chapter we discussed the use of crystals by shamans and healers. In addition to their use in this capacity, small crystal balls about the size of large marbles were often used as talismans or good luck charms. They were sometimes bound with wire or silver so that they could hang around one's neck as a pendant. This was popular in England during the Elizabethan era and even up to the nineteenth century. I have one of these pendants, which is pictured in the figure below.

All sizes and shapes of crystals continue to be used for divination, healing, meditation, and magic. In fact, now more than ever before there seems to be more of an interest in the metaphysical and psychic properties of crystals. Are we becoming more in tune with nature or becoming more spiritual, thus allowing us to recognize how important crystals are in this regard? I know that today crystals are playing an important spiritual role in many people's lives. If you have not

Fig. 2.1. Small Victorian crystal ball worn as jewelry.
Photograph © John DeSalvo.

experimented with them, this may be a good time to start. In part 3 of this book I offer instructions with regard to scrying, meditating, and undertaking magical rituals with crystals. I hope you will benefit from working with them and that the practice of so doing will enhance your life.

3
Psychic Studies
of Quartz Crystal

Why has quartz crystal been the mineral of choice since ancient times for use in metaphysical and psychic work, including divination? Is there a special quality or inherent property about quartz that gives it a special power? There must be something more to it than just its physical beauty. Diamonds and other gems are just as beautiful as quartz, and, in fact, some are even more aesthetically pleasing but have not been used to the extent quartz has in psychic and metaphysical work.

DOES QUARTZ CRYSTAL HAVE PSYCHIC PROPERTIES?

I personally believe that quartz crystals contain a special psychic property, which allows for a spiritual connection with higher realms and beings, and even the presence of God Himself. It may not make sense to most people that an ordinary rock could accomplish these things, but quartz crystal is no ordinary rock.

CRYSTAL DIVINATION

I would like to share with you some of my own experiments using crystals for divination, specifically pendulum divination. My experience with pendulum dowsing, or divination, goes back about fifteen years. Looking to have some fun with my two young sons, I bought a crystal pendulum game set called Kreskin's Krystal, named after the Amazing Kreskin. I found it in a thrift store. I had never used a pendulum before, and I believe that this one was made of reconstituted crystal.

We set up the game on our dining room table, and I followed the directions by asking questions and seeing which way the pendulum would swing. If it swung front to back, the answer to the question posed was yes. If it swung from side to side, the answer was no. I was amazed that when I initially picked up the pendulum and held it between my fingers it started moving like it had a life of its own! So, I thought, this is going to be fun! My older son started asking questions, and it moved either yes or no with much movement and vigor in response. It was amazing that the answers it offered up were correct. Then my other son began to ask questions. I felt like I was losing control, and it started to freak me out, as the expression goes, that this thing was moving by some outside force and also that it was very accurate.

My first thought was to stop using it because I didn't want my children to be exposed to any strange or unknown forces. I had bought it solely as a game and had no idea that it could be a real psychic tool. I quickly packed it up, much to the chagrin of my boys, who began to yell at me. They still had questions they wanted to ask it. However, I persisted and took it downstairs to the basement where I hid it under some boxes. Years later, I decided I wanted to try it again but could never find it.

This past year I decided to maybe try again and kept a lookout for a special pendulum. I had a friend give me one as a gift, but it didn't move like the first one had. Then I happened to visit a large antique mall. I was ready to leave when a locked cabinet (that rotates the shelves when you press a button) seemed to call to me.

I went over, and as I was rotating the shelves I saw a silver, Celtic-style pendulum that looked like it was an antique. I asked one of the clerks if I could look at it. When I held it in my hand it had the same response as the first crystal pendulum. I asked it if I should buy it, and it moved almost instantaneously to say yes! I bought it and decided to test it as scientifically as I could. I wanted to rule out that I was controlling the pendulum with my subconscious mind.

Here is what I did. I selected four playing cards, one from a red suit and three from the black suits. I shuffled them so I would not know which were the black ones and which was the red one and put them face down on the table. Then I swung the pendulum over each one and asked the question, "Is this the red card?" It was interesting that I would get only one yes answer, and that would almost always be the red card! Because I did not know which one the red card was, I believe I could not have subconsciously picked it out. Thus, I didn't control the swinging of the pendulum.

I did another experiment in which I used five cards, one to five. I shuffled them so again I would not know which card was which. I then picked one out and placed it on the table. Thus I had no idea if it was the one, two, three, four, or five card. I then swung the pendulum over the card and said, "Is this a one card?" and on up the line, up to five. It would always swing yes over only one of the numbers, and it was usually correct in identifying the number of this card.

I did this many times, and the success was phenomenal. I did not calculate the probability, but it was definitely way above chance. Since in these experiments I did not know what the cards were, I concluded that I did not influence the results of the experiment. Was another force or intelligence involved? Who knows, but I certainly felt something was controlling the movements. My point is that I believe pendulum divination is a psychic tool that works if one has a natural ability for it. It is similar to water dowsing, in that some people have a natural ability or talent for this and many do not.

Does a pendulum made of quartz crystal have any advantage over a non-quartz crystal pendulum? My experience shows that it does not. The best advice is to try many pendulums and find the one that responds the best for you. You will know right away.

My speculation as to why quartz may be superior to any other type of material for a pendulum is because of its piezoelectric property; it can produce a positive and negative charge on its surface when pressure is applied to it, like a battery. The positive and negative charges that result from this piezoelectric action may have some kind of correlation with a yes and no answer. Maybe the crystal gives off an aura as Frank Dorland observed in his study of the Mitchell-Hedges crystal skull, and this interacts with the user's aura. No one really knows how all this works, and it obviously needs more studies that use a scientific and analytical approach.

Experimenting with a pendulum might be fun for you. Once you find a pendulum that you feel responds to you, try the card experiments and improvise others to convince yourself that you are not influencing its movement, at least to the extent of knowing the answer to the experiment. Obviously, our muscles are moving the pendulum under some type of influence and the likely candidates are our subconscious, some unknown force, or spiritual entities. The cause has not yet been determined.

THE USE OF PSYCHICS IN SCIENTIFIC RESEARCH

I would now like to address the use of psychics in my research. It is important for me to discuss this, because later in the book several psychics will give their psychic impressions of an ancient crystal skull that I have been studying scientifically. My research colleagues know that traditionally I have been very skeptical about using psychics in research projects, but they also know that I am very open-minded and consider all possibilities. I believe that using psychics in research projects is valid, but one needs to apply some scientific and statistical methods to evaluate what they say.

Plate 1. This ancient cylinder seal (on the left), made from quartz crystal and dating from approximately 4000 BCE, was found in Mesopotamia. The line drawings on it indicate it may have been used as a talisman. (Featured on the right is a sample of the seal's imprint. The seal was rolled on a piece of wet clay and then dried.) Photograph © John DeSalvo.

Plate 2. The late Nick Nocerino, crystal skull expert and founder of the first society of crystal skulls. Nick was very psychic and studied crystals and crystal skulls, using both a scientific and psychic approach. Photograph courtesy of Khrys Nocerino.

Plate 3. A large altar crystal, owned by Nick Nocerino, which he gave to the author. Photograph © John DeSalvo.

Plate 4. A small, modern crystal skull, which was given to the author by Nick Nocerino. The author named it Max Jr. This crystal skull was in the possession of Nick for many years and he used it in his travels. It is from Madagascar. Photograph © John DeSalvo.

Plate 5. A beautiful quartz crystal specimen. Quartz has mesmerized humans throughout time. Photograph courtesy of Seann Xenja (www.dynamicenergycrystals.com).

Plate 6. A crystal ball, one of the oldest forms of divination known to man. Photograph © John DeSalvo.

7

8

Plates 7–12. Various types of quartz crystal: Smoky quartz crystal (plate 7); Rose quartz crystal (plates 8–10); Amethyst (plate 11); Citrine (plate 12). Photographs courtesy of Seann Xenja.

9

Plate 13. Scott Wolter with his large agate collection. Photograph © John DeSalvo.

Plate 14. Very old Native American carved agate in the form of animal totems. Photograph © John DeSalvo.

Plate 15. Polished quartz with rutile phantoms and inclusions. Photograph courtesy of Seann Xenja.

Plate 16. Another example of rutilated quartz. Photograph courtesy of Seann Xenja.

Plate 17. Although Herkimer crystals are a type of quartz crystal, they are different from most quartz crystals in that they are double-terminated. This is due to the fact that as they form they are not anchored to any base, enabling the crystal to grow on both ends. Photograph courtesy of Terry Roses.

Plate 18. A leather pouch made expressly to carry sacred crystals that were used in Native American healing ceremonies. This pouch is from the Black Elk collection, owned by Terry Roses. Photograph courtesy of Terry Roses.

Plate 19. The famous Mitchell-Hedges crystal skull, allegedly found in 1923 in the Mayan ruins in Lubaantun, Belize, is made of clear quartz and weighs approximately ten pounds. At one time it was known as the "Skull of Doom." Photograph courtesy of Khrys Nocerino.

Plate 20. Crystal skull expert Nick Nocerino discovered this crystal skull, ShaNaRa, during an archaeological dig in Mexico in 1995. Today his daughter Michele is its caretaker; she tours with it and uses it for healing. Most experts consider it to be an ancient crystal skull. Photograph courtesy of Michele Nocerino.

Plate 21. The Amethyst crystal skull weighs approximately eight pounds. Allegedly owned by Porfiro Diaz, president of Mexico from 1877–1911, its current whereabouts are thought to be in the United States, although its exact location is unknown. Photograph courtesy of Khrys Nocerino.

Plate 22. Small Himalayan crystal skull owned by the author. Photograph © John DeSalvo.

Plates 23–25. The crystal skull known as HeartStar, owned by Elizabeth HeartStar Keller of Arizona. This crystal skull is one of the eight small Himalayan skulls known as the star children of the Himalayas; it is very similar to one owned by the author. Plate 23 photograph courtesy of Nancy Bartell; plates 24 and 25 photographs courtesy of Kristin Reed.

24

25

Plate 26. The large crystal skulls brought to the United States by Frank Loo are displayed here on a table in the home of Nick Nocerino. Photograph courtesy of Khrys Nocerino.

Plate 27. The beautiful crystal collection of the late Gary Butler. He was responsible for scientifically testing the coating of a small Himalayan crystal skull. Photograph courtesy of Lynn Johnson.

Plate 28. Ann Hall's collection of crystals used in her psychometry work, which includes criminal cases. When working on a missing person's case, she uses a pendulum; for focus she uses a crystal ball; and for celestial help she uses fluorite. Photograph courtesy of Ann Hall.

Plate 29. Digital microscopy of top skull surface defects magnified three hundred times. Photograph courtesy of Scott Wolter.

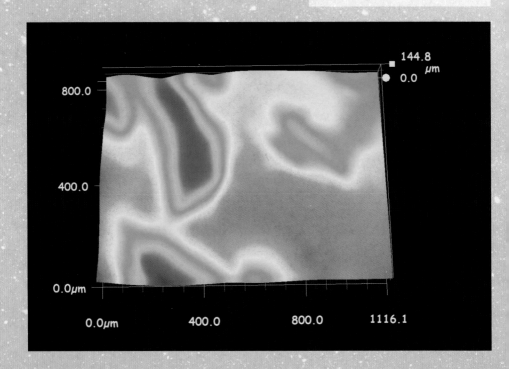

Many psychics merely give general information and don't reveal anything specific that later could be proved or validated. I want to work with psychics who can obtain specific information about things or events that can be confirmed and verified with facts. It's important for me to state that I only work with psychics who I have personally known for many years and who I have come to trust. Also, I have never paid psychics in any of my research projects so there is no conflict of interest. I want to keep the research as objective as possible and free of any agenda or selfish interest. The psychics I have chosen to use in my projects are the best I have encountered in more than thirty years of working in this area.

I usually use at least two psychics in a study and also compare their responses to each other and statistically attempt to calculate their accuracy and correspondence. Thus, if two psychics independently describe or say the same thing, it is much more credible, in my opinion, than just one. Also I want details and specifics and not generalities from the psychics. Two psychics described an antiquity that I was holding, and they both did it precisely, with minute details. That is very impressive, and if you calculated the improbability of this, it would be extremely high. Statistical analysis is the best one could do, because psychic phenomena are not repeatable and thus cannot be subjected to the same scientific method as physical objects. Psychic phenomena occur randomly, like quantum mechanics, so other standards and methods of evaluation need to be applied.

Today too many people claim to be psychic and say that they can tell you things about your crystal skull or some other object. How do we evaluate their psychic visions or perceptions? How do we know if there is any validity to their psychic impressions and claims? Are these people just imagining all these things, and are these visions just subconscious thoughts coming to the surface? Or is there something to this that is real and objective?

Psychic phenomena doesn't always follow the physical laws of our universe, like matter and energy do. Basically, you get repeatability in the physical world with regard to physical phenomena. In fact, physics is based on finding the laws that all objects obey. Let me give you an example. If you drop a steel ball from a high tower, no matter who measures it or when, it always falls at a constant acceleration of thirty-two feet per second squared. You can drop a ball anywhere on this planet, and it will always fall at this acceleration rate. This is the acceleration rate of a falling object in a vacuum; you must take air resistance and the rotation of the Earth, which is minimal, into account, but essentially the rate at which an object falls is always the same, and it is a repeatable phenomenon.

This is not so with psychic phenomena. Psychic phenomena are very seldom repeatable. We cannot use the same rigorous experimental approach, but we can use statistics and apply some of the scientific methods to this area, as we will see when we discuss psychometry.

Psychometry is one area of psychic research in which certain individuals have the ability or gift to hold an object in his or her hands and be able to ascertain specific information about its past history and information about its previous owners. Psychometrists are sometimes used by law enforcement investigators to find missing persons and kidnapping victims. In either of these cases, the psychometrist will usually hold some article of clothing that was owned by the victim, or something they possessed, to try to get psychic information about their current whereabouts. We will apply psychometry to our studies of ancient crystal skulls and compare this with the scientific data accumulated about a specific ancient crystal skull in a future chapter.

Because there is not that repeatability factor with psychic phenomena, it's more difficult to apply the scientific method to test it; however, it is not impossible, as we will see. That brings me to the question that has been confronting me for many years, ever since I went into psychic and paranormal research. How do you know that what a psychic is telling you is something that they are actually picking up from the object and is real and is not derived from their subconscious or imagination?

I have been using a very simple method in my psychic research. I work with two psychics who I regard very highly.* Each one conducts an independent examination of the object in question, and then each one tells me all they can about it. I then compare what they tell me with what I know about the object: its physical description and known history, for example. I also then compare the similarity of each psychic's description. If both give the same details about an object, and their descriptions are fairly similar, that is statistically good because it would appear that they are independently picking up accurate information about the object. The amount of detail makes a difference: its size, shape, color, composition, and its history, its age, and the period or culture it came from. I also ask them to give me spiritual or psychic information about it. Psychometry can be done in one of several ways. The psychics may hold the object, look at a picture of it, or just sense the information from a distance without actually viewing the object.

I am discussing all of this now, because later in the book I will be reporting on the psychometry that these psychics have done on an alleged ancient crystal skull that I have been scientifically testing. The information will hopefully confirm or contradict what we have determined scientifically and thus will give us added information about this crystal skull. Therefore, it's very important that you too know a little about these psychics, their unusual psychic abilities, and their high level of accuracy.

Psychic Becky Andreasson

The first psychic is Becky Andreasson. If the name Andreasson sounds familiar to you it's because Becky's mother, Betty Andreasson, is one of the most well-known and well-documented UFO abductees of all

---

*I want to make it clear that I personally know many psychics who are very good and have high accuracy rates, so I don't mean to exclude any of them with these statements. I selected two psychics to be part of my research studies because I have known them personally for many years and they have generously offered to donate their time to my research. In addition, my research is mainly in the area of psychometry, which is the forte of these women psychics.

time.[1] Becky has one of the highest levels of psychic ability of anyone I have ever known. In fact, she keeps herself away from the public because she is so good that years ago many people tried to contact her for readings. She doesn't do this for a living, and the constant requests began to interfere with her personal life. It's interesting that Becky also claimed to have been abducted as a child, and this may have something to do with her unusually strong psychic ability. Let me tell you a story about her to illustrate what I mean.

I've been a book collector for more than thirty years and have thousands of books all over my home. Most are in the basement and garage, because I have no place to put them. I also have thousands of books at my son's home. Becky told me she liked a specific Bible, which she didn't have. I told her I had a copy that I wasn't using and that she could have it if I could find it. I searched my house trying to find this Bible, but to no avail. I then searched my son's home but didn't have any luck there either. I couldn't find it, but I knew I had it in one of the houses.

This was very frustrating, and the next time I spoke to her I told her that I couldn't find it. "Go down to your basement," she told me, "and when you enter you will see two piles of books in front of you. The pile to your left has the book in it; it is the third book down."

I told her I had already looked through those piles and it was not there. I was surprised she even knew I had two piles of books there, as she had never been in my basement. As soon as I got off the phone I went downstairs. I stood in front of both piles of books, removed the top two books from the left stack, and there was the Bible in question! For those who are skeptical, try calculating the odds of finding a specific book among thousands of books in two houses!

Psychic Helene Olsen

The other extremely gifted and talented psychic participating in my research is Helene Olsen. Helene is a psychic medium with a rare gift for psychometry. She's from Massachusetts and does readings professionally. She conducts monthly readings on several radio programs, which listeners can call in to. Helene, like Becky, is extremely accurate and has, on numerous occasions, described artifacts to me with astonishing accuracy. On several occasions she has told me the age of an enigmatic artifact, the culture it was from, its purpose, and how it was used.

It's very fascinating that Helene and Becky agree on their psychometric readings about 75 percent of the time, which also tells me they are correct in the information they are obtaining. Thus I have two very talented and gifted psychometrists participating in my research projects. This is excellent for analysis and statistical purposes.

CONCLUSIONS

Not everyone has access to gifted and talented psychics, so what does the average person who wants to find out psychic information about their crystals, crystal skulls, or artifacts do? My suggestion is to experiment and try to validate what you see or feel. Also understand that what you see may not be real but may spring from your own mind or subconscious. Trust your intuition and, with practice, you may develop a real skill and talent for psychometry and/or seeing visions in crystals (scrying). An entire chapter in this book is devoted to scrying; in it I give you suggestions and tips on how to scry with crystals and other objects.

Crystals can also help us to face and learn about our subconscious. My speculation is that crystals amplify thoughts, both good and bad, and thus they can be used as a microscope for self-inspection. You must be careful as you do not want to expose or bring out into the conscious mind too much information too soon. It may cause you problems, because it may be difficult to integrate the information being presented all at once. However, if we can identify our inner thoughts and determine what is driving us unconsciously, we may learn how to deal better with our problems and attitudes.

I personally find it very helpful to learn about my motivations, values, and hidden thoughts. It's an experience that's not always enjoyable but usually very enlightening, and sometimes it explains my behavior and past actions. It's very revealing, and I believe it's a good tool to use to "know thyself," as Socrates would say. It can give us a better understanding of the world and how to deal with it successfully.

4
Quartz Crystals
in Healing

For decades there have been innumerable books written on the healing properties of quartz crystals and other minerals. They have been very popular, especially with natural-healing advocates. Suggestions on how to use or apply the crystals for healing have been many and varied. The simplest and most popular method is to hold the crystal in your hand while you rest or meditate, or you can place it on the afflicted parts of your body. Another method is to rest it on one of the seven chakras, the spiritual energy centers of the human body.

Some people have claimed to be able to heal with quartz at a distance. The healer holds a crystal in her hand and thinks about or visualizes the affected person. They then send out healing energy to that person at a distance, using the crystal as a transmitter and an amplifier.

I first heard about this when I was in graduate school decades ago, and I shrugged it off and dismissed it. I was a scientist, and I believed in hard data. (I believed then, and I still do, that one should consult their medical doctor for any troubling physical symptoms.) All this stuff about an inert rock healing the body seemed ridiculous and just one more of the so-called New Age techniques that had no basis in fact, and when put to the scientific test it would be shown to be invalid.

The only problem with my conclusion is that there were many people who claimed to have been healed with crystals. Not only were people claiming that physical healing was taking place, but mental and/or psychological healing as well. It was hard to dismiss this as imagination because of the number of claims. Well, like any good scientist, I decided to investigate this in my own way. I tried holding different types of materials, which included various common rocks, minerals, gems, and, of course, quartz crystals.

I cannot say I was ever physically healed by any of them, but when I meditated with the quartz crystals I definitely felt a sense well-being and a greater contentment with myself and others. As mentioned in the previous chapter, the crystal seemed to act as an amplifier for my thoughts and emotions, in a good way. I would see some of my faults or actions as they really were, and this gave me the courage to try to amend them. It also gave me a clearer perspective of my spiritual being and the spiritual path I was on. I did realize that much of this could be a placebo effect or possibly wishful thinking, so I put the crystals on the shelf to investigate at some point in the future.

I was studying mathematics at that time. The math equations we were using included many theoretical dimensions, so I had a thought that maybe crystals were unique in that they existed in many dimensions (some we cannot perceive) and we can only see them by their projection into our three-dimensional, space-time world.

Let's explore this further, together.

RESONANCE

First we will look at resonance, which may be the most important factor in how crystals operate, both on the physical and spiritual level. *Resonance* is defined as ability or tendency of a system to oscillate or vibrate at one specific frequency more than another. For example, each string of a guitar vibrates at a different frequency, depending on its length. These specific frequencies are known as the resonant frequencies of the system being discussed. It's a transferring of energy between one system and another. Even Galileo recognized and studied the resonance of musical strings—and also of pendulums—in the seventeenth century. It's also important to realize that there are many types of resonance, not just acoustic, but also mechanical and electrical.

Let's take the example of soldiers walking across a bridge. If the soldiers march in step and their frequency is the same as the bridge, the bridge will start to vibrate and may collapse. Historically, as a result, when soldiers crossed man-made bridges they were told to walk out of step. We also know that sound can shatter glass and crystal. A high-pitched trumpet can sometimes shatter a glass, as can a high-pitched vocal sound. If you strike a tuning fork so that it vibrates and put another similar tuning fork near it, the second tuning fork will begin to vibrate at the same frequency as the first; energy has been transferred from one to the other. There are numerous examples of resonance, and these are only a few.

How does this relate to healing with crystals? Many people, myself included, believe that we are composed of both a physical and a spiritual body. In all the cases above, we are talking about physical resonance, but could there be such a thing as spiritual resonance? Some people refer to this spiritual essence as our soul.

And can a physical resonance produce a corresponding resonance in the spiritual realm, which in turns affects our spiritual body? As an example, assume that the first tuning fork is in the physical realm, but the second is in the spiritual. Somehow, the vibrations from the physical realm influence the spiritual.

Some people might ask how this notion of a physical and spiritual resonance affects healing, and I would argue that this could be one component of it. For example, if you had a problem with a specific part of your body, maybe the crystal could resonate at that frequency and activate something physical in that part or produce some type of physical healing vibration. As far as I know, this has never been measured or tested scientifically. The problem is that since tissue is composed of so many components, you would have to get all of them resonating together, which would be unlikely. Also, the amplitude would be negligible. So, even though there may be a physical component to this resonance from the crystals, I do not think it would be significant. Again, I could be wrong and this needs to be tested, but this is my opinion based on what I know about physical resonance.

What about the spiritual aspect of this? Unfortunately, this also has never been measured, and I do not know how this could be done at this time in our technology. Maybe we will develop more sophisticated equipment in the future that will be able to measure spiritual energies and spiritual resonance, but for now we cannot. Perhaps the most sophisticated technology that we have at present to measure a variable of this sort is the equipment that ghost hunters use—a device called an EMF meter, which calibrates the energy fields of ghosts. Actually, it measures a change so when a ghost is present, they upset the normal electromagnetic field of the environment. The changed field is then measured with this device. I own and have used this device for ghost hunting, and it's proved to be a very interesting and valuable piece of equipment. Perhaps someday a device will be invented that could somehow measure spiritual vibrations and resonance.

Conversely, is it possible that spiritual healing can affect physical healing? I heard many years ago that illness first appears in the spiritual body and then manifests to the physical. A clairvoyant or psychic would first see something dark or wrong in the person's spiritual aura. Initially, the person may experience no symptoms, but after a period of weeks or months, physical symptoms develop. Thus, true healing may be spiritual and this would then affect or heal the physical. Thus this would be a mechanism of how crystal healing could take place. Again, we have no evidence for this, and I do not suggest this as a healing or diagnostic method.

Let's look at a theoretical example. We start with a normal, healthy person. All of a sudden there is an abnormality in some region of his spiritual body. Maybe the aura is weak, or dark, or is of a different color in that area of the body. Those psychics who can read auras believe this indicates a disease process starting to occur. Many years ago I wrote a book called *Andrew Jackson Davis, First American Prophet and Clairvoyant* about the nineteenth-century clairvoyant and prophet. Davis was also a medical doctor and claimed he could see people's auras and make a medical diagnosis based on what he saw, without any physical examination or tests.[1] In my book I document these claims and link the famous prophet and seer Edgar Cayce with Andrew Jackson Davis. Cayce's own son found their similarities to be uncanny.[2] It could be argued that Davis was Edgar Cayce's predecessor in that he was able to make a diagnosis by analyzing a person's aura, which Cayce would also do many years later.

THE USE OF CRYSTAL FOR HEALING PURPOSES

I must be honest and say that I never had any luck using quartz crystals—or for that matter any gem, mineral, rock, or relic—for healing, and I am not an advocate of this type of healing method. This is because I have not seen significant statistical results. I don't want to give you the idea that spiritual healing doesn't exist. I truly believe that God and the angels can and do heal people at their will and miraculously. The problem is that this type of healing does not happen very frequently; statistics of people being healed in this way are not promising.

I do, however, believe that prayer can assist with healing, but in a slower and more conservative way. Allow me to clarify: I am not saying that spontaneous healing through prayer doesn't happen. It *may* occur, but it's very rare, perhaps one in a hundred thousand or a million cases. Documented cases in the Catholic Church exist; they are of rare spontaneous healings at religious sites such as Lourdes and Fatima. We all know the power of prayer and the energy it releases. Maybe it works by strengthening one's spiritual body, and this is what facilitates healing.

Given all of this, I *did* have my own personal experience with spiritual healing, and I will relay it to you here. For some time I was very involved with the charismatic movement in the Catholic Church and even sponsored "Life in the Spirit" programs. I was also a member of a local charismatic group that conducted healing sessions for church members and others. If you have ever attended one of these healing sessions, you know how easy it is to get carried away by the excitement they generate.

My experience took place one summer, just before I was going to begin a full-time position as director of religious education at a Catholic church. An uncle of mine in New York, who was involved in the charismatic movement, invited me to come and meet a friend of his who was a pastor and well known for his charismatic healing ability. At that time I had no knowledge about charismatic healing. Well, after we talked for some time I mentioned to the pastor that I never had had a significant spiritual experience. His reply was, "You will," and with that, he told me to stand up. I had no idea what he was going to do, but I followed his directions. He then placed his hands several inches above my head and started praying in a strange language, which I thought was very weird. However, I just stood silently. All of a sudden I felt a lot of heat and warmth enter my head and move down my body.

Then, abruptly, I felt as if a train had hit me—I was propelled back instantly. The pastor had never touched me. My uncle, who was standing behind me, fortunately caught me. I guess this was standard operating practice, and my uncle was prepared. I had no idea this would happen; I had never been to or in a charismatic healing session before. I was completely stunned! As a scientist and a rational person, what had happened to me was not logical. The heat coming from above—when the pastor had *not* been touching my head—and then a strange force pushing me backward, was most difficult to understand and to explain.

My uncle and aunt were smiling at my confusion. But there was more. The next thing the pastor did was to come up to me and say: "Jesus wants me to heal your back." I had hurt my back several months before when I lifted my daughter into a swing at the park. It was nothing serious, but it had been bothering me and I had to exercise caution when lifting things. The pastor picked up both of my legs while holding my feet, and I felt what seemed to be electricity running up my legs and into my body. When he was done I stood up, and my back was healed. I have never had a problem in that location again.

I also had another aliment, which I asked the pastor to heal. He prayed over me but to no avail. Why? This is the mystery of healing. Why are some people healed and not others? Why is one thing healed in a person while something else is not?

This is the mystery of God's will.

I do believe Jesus healed my back that day.

CONCLUSIONS

I want to clarify my views on healing with crystals. I believe that healing with crystals, as we know it today, is ineffective and does not produce any significant physical healing. That's why I believe it to be a false healing science. On the other hand, I do believe that *meditating* with crystals can help your peace of mind and maybe even give you a measure of spiritual insight and comfort.

Does that mean that physical healing with crystals is a dead topic? The ancients claimed to be able to heal with crystals, and many people believe they were successful. Fundamentally I believe that a true practice of using crystals to heal does exist or did exist yet has been lost or is only known to a few people to whom the secret was passed down. Unless it's discovered or rediscovered, and proved to be successful, I do not give any credibility at this time to physical healing with crystals.

A good analogy is the following. Let's say you give a primitive tribe a bottle of penicillin and tell them it cures infections, but you do not tell them how to use it (by injecting it into the patient). Without having been given the specific method, primitive man may try different things, such as holding the bottle over a sick person and perhaps chanting a few incantations. Or he might rub it on his body and do all sorts of other things with it, but it has no effect because it needs to be injected into the patient to be effective.

I believe the same holds true for healing with crystals. They hold a power to heal, but modern crystal practitioners have not unlocked the lock. Maybe someday we will find the enigmatic key and the hidden knowledge will surface, to the benefit of us all.

PART TWO

— ✶ —

All about
Crystal Skulls

5
The Ancient Crystal Skulls

When I am asked, "What is a crystal skull?" I usually begin by saying, "It is a piece of quartz crystal that is carved in the shape of a human skull." I am not trying to be funny but its name tells you exactly what it is. I suppose there are numerous shapes that can be carved out of quartz, so why is the shape of the human skull so important? What is its significance?

Today the skull symbolizes many things. It symbolizes poisonous or toxic chemicals and is also used as a symbol of death. Pirate ships flew flags featuring a skull and crossbones as a symbol of power as they intimidated and terrorized those they pursued on the high seas. Secret societies also used the skull in their initiations. I remember in one of the secret initiations I was in many years ago, a human skull was used to illustrate that life is fleeting and death certain; this underscored the fact that friendship and brotherhood are the most important things in this world. With the new gothic look today, the skull has received a revival; it is featured in jewelry, tattoos, and earrings.

One of my favorite stories about skulls—which I watched on *The History Channel*—involves Nostradamus. We don't know if it's true, but it's interesting nonetheless. Allegedly, Nostradamus was buried with a plaque that stated the exact day and year that his tomb would be opened. Before he died, he said that whoever held his skull in their hands and drank from it would gain all his knowledge and power. During the French Revolution three soldiers happened to discover his tomb. When they entered it they found a plaque with that exact date on it. One of the soldiers picked up Nostradamus's skull and proudly drank from it. Immediately, a stray bullet came from nowhere and went through his head and killed him.[1]

The symbol of the skull plays a role in our present culture and in ancient ones as well. Why did some ancient cultures decide to carve quartz crystal in the form of a human skull in the first place? There have been many suggestions and theories, the main one being that it was due to quartz crystal's beauty and aesthetically pleasing effect. I, however, believe there is a different reason.

The time and effort for an ancient culture to carve a human-size crystal skull from a solid piece of crystal, without modern tools and

Fig. 5.1. Crystal skull enthusiast Zane Grant with the crystal skull Akator.
Akator weights three hundred and fifty pounds and is a smoky quartz
skull carved by famed Brazilian master carver Geraldo Leandro de Souza.
Photograph courtesy of Zane Grant.

equipment, is mind-boggling. A scientist at Hewett-Packard, after studying the Mitchell-Hedges crystal skull, said he believed that it was carved and polished by hand. This would have taken more than three hundred years to complete.[2] There had to be more important reasons to produce the crystal skulls than just for the purpose of decoration, beauty, or art.

It is interesting that whenever I get into a conversation with someone on various subjects, inevitably the subject of crystal skulls comes up, and I am always asked if I have seen any crystal skulls lately. Then the next question I am usually asked is how many known ancient crystal skulls are there and can I describe them. This is a difficult question because there is no real consensus on which of the famous crystal skulls are really ancient and which are just old or modern.

To give you an example, at one time the crystal skull in the Smithsonian Institution and the one in the British Museum were both accepted by most crystal skull researchers as being ancient. But in the 1990s tests done at the British Museum showed that they were carved in the mid-nineteenth century and thus are not ancient. We will discuss these tests later.

As we mentioned earlier, we know that a crystal skull cannot be scientifically dated because it's made of silicon, not carbon. Thus, we can't use carbon-14 dating on them. With the crystal skulls we currently are aware of, and as stated earlier, the best we could do would be to show that there are no modern tool marks on them. Examples of modern tooling include the use of rotary wheels (although some ancient cultures had primitive versions of this), laser or ion beams, or other modern equipment. If any of these marks are found on a crystal skull we would conclude that the skull is a modern production. Also, if any chemical abrasives that were not available in ancient times are detected, and if they are of modern origin and were used to polish it, we would also conclude that the skull in question is modern.

If we made a list of the well-known crystal skulls that are the most probable candidates for being ancient, we would come up with about half a dozen or so. In this chapter we will discuss only the ancient crystal skulls that are accepted as ancient by a majority of crystal skull researchers. I am sure there are others that some people claim to be ancient, but we will focus on the accepted ones or the ones that have been in the public view for some time.

ANCIENT CRYSTAL SKULLS

Crystal skulls commonly understood to be ancient include the Mitchell-Hedges skull, ShaNaRa, the Amethyst crystal skull, and the Mayan crystal skull.* I would also like to include a brief discussion of both the British Museum and Smithsonian skulls as they are both well-known and were at one time accepted as being ancient. I will also discuss the Paris crystal skull before ending with a discourse about the alleged ancient crystal skull named Max.

You may be curious as to why each crystal skull has its own unique name and how it got its name. Usually an owner or caretaker of a crystal skull will name it based on some information they have about it, such as the location where it was found, its appearance, composition, or color. Another way a crystal skull may get its name is that sometimes the ancient skulls name *themselves*. The perceptive or psychic owner of the skull will hear the name psychically or audibly. This is what happened in the case of Max and JoAnn Parks, its keeper, as articulated in the foreword of this book.

As we will see, the origin of many of the ancient crystal skulls are claimed to be pre-Columbian, Mesoamerican artifacts in that it's claimed they were found in Mayan or Aztec ruins in Mexico and Central America. Some recent ones that have come to public attention are from China, Tibet, and other parts of Asia. Could these skulls be on the order of thousands to tens of thousands of years old? Could they have magical or psychic powers that can be tapped in to? Some people

---

*There is also a group of skulls that has the strong potential to be ancient. These are known as the small Himalayan crystal skulls; they will be discussed in the next chapter.

allege that they are storage devices and, as such, hold records of past ancient civilizations.

I will now list and briefly discuss all the known and accepted ancient crystal skulls.

The Mitchell-Hedges Crystal Skull

The Mitchell-Hedges crystal skull is the most famous of all the ancient crystal skulls. (For another photograph of this skull please see plate 19 of the color insert.) This skull is made of clear quartz and weighs approximately ten pounds. It closely resembles the size and shape of a human skull and, in fact, its jawbone is removable. It was allegedly discovered in 1923 by the British explorer F. A. Mitchell-Hedges. He claimed to have found it in Mayan ruins in Lubaantun, Belize (called British Honduras at that time).[3] A conflicting story claims that his adopted daughter, Anna, discovered it on her seventeenth birthday while looking through the Mayan ruins with her father. At one time it was known as "The Skull of Doom."

Fig. 5.2. Nick Nocerino with the Mitchell-Hedges crystal skull.
Photograph courtesy of Khrys Nocerino.

There has been some controversy regarding the age and provenance of this crystal skull. Some self-proclaimed crystal skull experts say it was manufactured in Germany in the middle nineteenth or early twentieth century and that Mitchell-Hedges did not find it in Lubaantun but acquired it at an auction.[4] Some people believe it is a female, due to its smaller size and other distinct features. We will discuss the tests that were done on this skull in chapter 8. There has been much paranormal activity reported around this crystal skull, and I will recount one of those stories now.[5]

At one time Anna Mitchell-Hedges had loaned the skull to Frank Dorland, a well-known art conservator and museum consultant. One evening an invited guest of Dorland's showed up at his house with a well-known Satanist to see the skull. This Satanist asked to see the skull, claiming that it had been produced by Satan and thus it belonged to him as he was Satan's representative on Earth. He also said it was an energy source for the powers of darkness and that it was to be used for evil purposes. Of course, Dorland did not give the skull to him and was relieved when this person left.

Dorland claims that in his house that night there was much poltergeist phenomena (moving of physical objects spontaneously by some unknown force or power), and in the morning they discovered that kitchen utensils, a phone, and other small objects were strewn all over the place. Strange noises had also been heard throughout the night, including human voices, bells, and bouncing sounds like Ping-Pong balls. Dorland believed this poltergeist phenomenon was due to a clashing of positive and negative energies between the Satanist and the skull.

I don't know whether Dorland allowed the Satanist to handle the skull or not, but perhaps the mere presence of this person was responsible for setting off this chain of events. Dorland did say that after this experience he never allowed anyone to hold or touch the skull, which implies that he may have allowed this Satanist to hold it. According to Dorland, this was the only disturbing experience he ever had with the crystal skull.

Dorland reported many interesting types of psychic phenomena during the time he had the skull in his possession. He not only saw strange visions in it (see chapter 9 on scrying), but he heard beautiful music and bells emanating from it, as well as human chanting. At one time Dorland claims to have seen a large halo around the skull that lasted for more than five minutes. Dorland believed that these effects were produced only through human interaction with the skull and would not happen to the skull in isolation. It's my opinion that the skull has its own energy, as does the person who is interacting with it. The intersection of these energies is what generates the above-referenced phenomena. This is very similar to quantum theory in which the observer affects the outcome of the results of an experiment, leading me to believe that both quantum physics and string theory may be in effect here.

Other stories, which cannot be corroborated, allege that the skull has caused the deaths of persons that may have abused it verbally or physically. Still other stories exist that attest to the good luck the skull has caused. All of these stories are unsupported, however, and without further evidence we can only accept them as conjecture. Later I will discuss a 2008 test by the Smithsonian Museum on the Mitchell-Hedges crystal skull that will shatter preconceived notions about it.

ShaNaRa

ShaNaRa is also made of clear quartz and weighs about thirteen pounds. It was discovered by Nick Nocerino during an archaeological dig in Mexico in 1995. He located it by using psychic archaeology (i.e., locating ancient ruins or artifacts by using psychic ability). After Nick passed away in 2004, Kirby Seid became its caretaker, although it is still owned by the Nocerino family. Recently, Nick's daughter Michele became its caretaker (please see plate 20 of the color insert). As such, she uses ShaNaRa for healing. Most crystal skull researchers consider ShaNaRa to be an authentic ancient crystal skull. He is made available to the public, most often during exhibits and conferences on crystal skulls.

Fig. 5.3. ShaNaRa. Photograph courtesy of Joan Rhodes.

The Amethyst Crystal Skull

The ancient Amethyst crystal skull is different from the other crystal skulls in that it is made of amethyst and, given that, it has a dark purple color. (Please see plate 21 of the color insert.) Amethyst is a violet variety of quartz crystal; its color is due to iron and aluminum impurities. This crystal skull is smaller than the others and only weighs about eight pounds. It is thought that Porfiro Diaz, who was president of Mexico in 1877 until he fled from office in 1911, owned this skull at one time and actually had it on his desk. After his stewardship, the skull remained with a family in Mexico until a Mayan priest and shaman, Francisco Reyes, bought the skull from them in the late 1970s. It was brought to the United States around the early 1980s, and rumor has it that some wealthy businessmen currently own the skull and have stored it in a safe in San Jose, California. It has also been called by the name Ami and was tested at the Hewlett-Packard labs, as was the previously mentioned Mitchell-Hedges skull.

The Mayan Crystal Skull

This is one of the most mysterious of all the ancient crystal skulls. It is composed of clear quartz and weighs about nine pounds. Its present location is unknown. Its origin is believed to be Honduras, where it was discovered in the late 1800s. There are different versions of where and when it was discovered. Rumor has it that it is currently being stored in Texas, but there is no proof of this.[6] The story of the incredible journey of the skull from Mexico to the United States is told by Richard

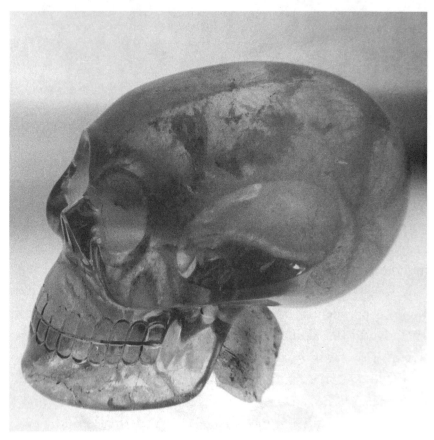

Fig. 5.4. The Mayan crystal skull.
Photograph courtesy of Khrys Nocerino.

Shafsky in the appendix. While this skull was in the United States, Nick Nocerino and Richard Shafsky studied and researched it together and brought it to Hewlett-Packard and Bell Labs in California for testing. The Hewlett-Packard tests show that this skull was carved against the axis of the crystal, which would be very difficult to do without shattering the quartz.

The British Museum Crystal Skull

The British Museum crystal skull takes its name from the location in which it is stored and displayed. It was considered to be an authentic ancient crystal skull until it was determined by British Museum tests done at their London laboratory in 1996 that it had been made with modern tools and is probably no older than the nineteenth century. The British Museum dropped it from the ancient crystal skull list, and the skull was reclassified as an antique or old skull.

The Smithsonian Crystal Skull

There was also a skull known as the Smithsonian crystal skull. It was named such because it first surfaced at the Smithsonian Institute, having been donated by an anonymous giver. It is extremely large and weighs thirty-one pounds and is fifteen inches high. It was carved using a substance known as carborundum, a modern abrasive. Experts believe it was carved within the past one hundred years, and thus it is now classified as a modern crystal skull. It is currently exhibited as a fake at the Museum of Natural History in Washington, D.C.

The Paris Crystal Skull

Another crystal skull, also originally thought to be ancient, is known as the Paris crystal skull. Tests carried out on it in France in 2007–2008, however, revealed evidence of polishing and abrasion by modern tools; therefore, it is no longer considered to be ancient. Current theory holds that it was carved in the eighteenth or nineteenth century.

Max

Max is also composed of clear quartz crystal and weighs about eighteen pounds. Its current caretaker is JoAnn Parks of Texas, and thus it is often referred to as the Texas crystal skull. (Please see the foreword for more information about Max and JoAnn Parks.) Max was originally discovered in Guatemala, but beyond that we know nothing of its origins. As mentioned earlier, it was given to an American-born Tibetan priest named Lama Norbu, who was residing in Guatemala at the time. He eventually gave it to JoAnn Parks. JoAnn travels extensively with Max to allow people to spend time with him. Like ShaNaRa, Max is made available to the public during exhibits and conferences on crystal skulls.

Most crystal skull enthusiasts believe Max is an authentic ancient crystal skull. In 1996 the British Museum studied Max but decided not to release the results of their testing. Up until last year I had never meditated with any of the well-known ancient crystal skulls. Because I don't think I'm psychic, I never had the motivation to try. It was fine just to talk to others about their experiences and talk to the caretakers of the skulls.

However, one day an old friend of mine, who currently lives in Arizona, e-mailed me to tell me that JoAnn Parks and Max were going to be in my area. I quickly contacted JoAnn, who told me that she hadn't realized I lived in Minnesota (this would be her second trip to my area). I scheduled a thirty-minute appointment to meditate with Max at the home where she was staying. I had never met JoAnn before, although we had known each other for years, having communicated through the Internet and over the telephone. I was really looking forward to meeting her and Max.

When I arrived we gave each other a big hug. JoAnn is one of the most gracious people I have ever met. She gives you the impression you are meeting a member of royalty, and at the same time she is very warm and down-to-earth. We talked about everything, including my crystal skull, which I brought for her to look at. It's interesting that several

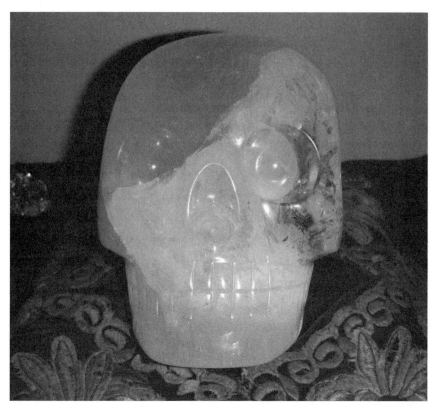

Fig. 5.5. Max, the ancient crystal skull.
Photograph © John DeSalvo.

other people visiting there wanted to see my crystal skull and hold it. Almost all of them said it had wonderful healing energy, and one person held it for about thirty minutes and did not want to give it up. JoAnn also loved it and said if I ever wanted to get rid of it, she would take it and keep it with Max.

When my time came to be with Max, JoAnn came into the small room with me, and Max was placed on a nicely decorated table with a chair in front of it for me to sit on. I asked JoAnn if it was okay to touch Max, and she said yes. I have to say that at this point I never expected to feel anything unusual or have any great experience. I brought my camera to take some pictures of him. I also had been told that information could be downloaded from Max to other skulls, so I brought along my two crystal skulls (Hapi and Max Jr.*) to place near Max.

When I walked up to Max and put my hands on him and I got a big shock. Yes, a real electric shock! And I jumped back. I put my hands on him again and felt a strong current of static electricity coming from him to me. I had never felt this with any other object I had touched, and especially not quartz crystals. Later JoAnn confirmed that she had seen me jump back in this way.

JoAnn then left the room, and I placed my skulls (both my modern one, Max Jr., and my Himalayan one, Hapi) near Max and just sat quietly and meditated for the rest of the time, which was extremely peaceful and restful. After that the time went by very quickly, and I took many photos of Max and my skulls near him. At the end of the half hour JoAnn came in to get me and we sat and talked for the next several hours with other people that were visiting.

LAWS OF NATURE NOT YET PROVED

I want to address the skeptic who doesn't believe in the paranormal or psychic ability. Many mysteries that seemed to be supernatural in past centuries have been shown to have a physical and scientific cause once the law of physics in which they operate was discovered. I believe this entire area of paranormal research will eventually be scientifically proved and explicable by a new law of physics yet to be discovered. I am also sure that quantum physics and superstring theory, two of my own particular interests, will play a role in this.

This calls to mind the interest in pyramid power in the 1970s, when

---

*In addition to Hapi (a small Himalayan crystal skull that we will discuss later), I had acquired a modern crystal skull from Nick Nocerino, who had given it to me as a gift before he passed away. He told me it had been in his possession for about ten years and he used it when he traveled. I was honored to own this personal treasure from Nick and still have it today. I named it "Max Jr." because he looked similar to the famous ancient crystal skull, Max, owned by JoAnn Parks. Nick told me that this crystal came from Madagascar, where excellent high-quality quartz crystal is mined.

everyone was experimenting with this phenomenon. It was believed that pyramids gave off some supernatural energy that could change objects (sharpen razor blades, preserve food, etc.) and be beneficial in meditation and healing. Several years ago I was contacted by Russian and Ukrainian researchers, many of whom were at the Institute of Physics in Ukraine. They informed me of their intention to release their ten years of pyramid research data to the West, which, in my opinion and that of others, proved the existence of a measurable energy field around pyramids.[7] Other research in the United States, specifically that of the American scientist and engineer Joe Parr, have confirmed much of this.[8]

What was once supernatural and mysterious is now explainable by science. Thus, I say, "Incredible discoveries are made because of incredible hypotheses." If you can imagine something, it may very well turn out to be true.

6
Ancient Himalayan Crystal Skulls and Dropa Discs

One of the first books ever published on crystal skulls was by my good friend Nick Nocerino, who I talk about throughout this book. When I first became interested in crystal skulls in 2001, his name didn't mean anything to me, but the book that he coauthored in 1988, *Mysteries of the Crystal Skulls Revealed,* definitely caught my attention.[1] Here was a person who approached this area of research very scientifically and logically. He also seemed to be a very credible individual.

One day I called Nick and he told me that he had some company: a gentlemen and his wife from Hong Kong. This was Mr. Frank Loo, an important person in our story. Frank had brought about fourteen life-size ancient skulls and a Dropa disc from China, which Nick was looking at and studying. I was fascinated by this and asked Nick if I could introduce myself to Frank and chat for a moment or two. Nick immediately put Frank on the phone, and he and I had a brief exchange and said we would contact each other again through e-mail. This started my short but very nice friendship with Frank Loo.

HAPI, MY HIMALAYAN CRYSTAL SKULL

I decided I would like to do some real scientific testing on an alleged ancient crystal skull. Frank appreciated my scientific expertise and sincere interest and agreed to try to find me one to test. Some short time later, he had one for me. It was a small crystal skull, about the size of a baseball, and it really looked ancient. Oddly enough, it was spotted with some red pigment. I didn't know what the pigment was at the time.

Fig. 6.1. The crystal skull that the author obtained from Frank Loo.
Photograph © John DeSalvo.

I call this skull Hapi; the story of how it got its name is interesting and is a good example of how skulls name themselves. Shortly after I got it I asked it what its name was, and after a period of time I started hearing the world "happy" every time I asked. I thought that couldn't be right, but I kept hearing that word. At first I was reluctant to call the skull Happy because I believed that my subconscious was generating the name due to the fact that the skull appeared to be smiling and therefore happy. Also I wanted it to have a more exotic or ancient-sounding name.

I shared all of this with my friend Linda Frisch, who is also psychic. She told me that Hapi was a god of the Nile. Maybe this god was somehow connected to my skull. Well, that put a whole new spin on things with the result being that, at the end of the day, I was more than happy to name my skull Hapi!

After I got Hapi, I sent it to Nick for his opinion. Unfortunately, I did not realize that he was very sick, and he never had a chance to look at it. Coincident with this, I had also become very involved

Fig. 6.2. My Himalayan crystal skull to the right of Max, and the crystal skull given to me by Nick Nocerino to the left of Max.
Photograph © John DeSalvo.

with other venues of scientific research that were demanding my full time and attention. Given this, I reluctantly told Frank Loo that I would have to put my interest in crystal skulls aside for the time being. He said he understood and wished me well with my other ventures.

I didn't know what Nick and Khrys would do with the skull, nor did I care. Fortunately for me, and as I found out later, Khrys just packed it up and placed it in her storage room or sewing room where it remained undisturbed for the next eight years, until I felt it was calling for me to get it back. I'm not sure what reignited my interest, but it was something from deep within me. Khrys and I had kept in touch after Nick passed away, and during one of our conversations I was going to ask her about the crystal skull but decided not to. If she had gotten rid of it, I didn't want her to feel bad if I asked for it back, so I said nothing. Almost psychically, right after our phone conversation, she e-mailed me and told me she still had my crystal skull. She also wanted to know if I would like it back or whether one of my sons would like it.

The first thing I did with the skull upon its return was to take many pictures of it at different angles and lighting and put them up on a password-protected page on my website for experts and friends to study and give me their opinion. (Please see plate 22 of the color insert for a picture of my skull.) Little did I know that one of my close friends and research colleague's wife, Jeanne Dunn, would come up with the first discovery leading to the identification of my crystal skull. She had collected crystals and modern crystal skulls for numerous years.

I sent her a photo of my crystal skull, and she told me right away that it looked very similar to another small crystal skull known as HeartStar, which was owned by Elizabeth HeartStar Keller of Arizona. Jeanne sent me pictures of HeartStar, and indeed they were extremely similar. (Please see plates 23–25 of the color insert.)

I found the website that Elizabeth had put together about

Fig. 6.3. Chris and Jeanne Dunn with Max in 2004.
Photograph courtesy of Jeanne Dunn.

Fig. 6.4. The large Himalayan skulls.
Photograph courtesy of Khrys Nocerino.

Fig. 6.5. Nick Nocerino psychically studies Frank Loo's crystal skulls.
Photograph courtesy of Khrys Nocerino.

HeartStar (www.astrojourneys.com/heartstar.html), and from it I learned about a group of eight small crystal skulls, known as the star children of the Himalayas. The story was that all of the skulls had been found together in the Tibetan Himalayas and carved by the same ancient culture.[2]

Frank Loo brought these small skulls to the United States in 2003 and found caretakers for them. Elizabeth believed that the skull Frank had given me was one of these eight Himalayan skulls and a photo on her website seemed to corroborate this, which she was very pleased about. Please keep in mind that Frank Loo first brought the large, life-size Himalayan crystal skulls (pictured in figure 6.4) to the home of Nick Nocerino several years before he distributed the eight small ones to caretakers around the world. I believe my small Himalayan crystal skull was the first one he gave out.

Even though I agreed with Elizabeth and felt it was obvious from the photo that my crystal skull was indeed one of the eight, I also felt it was important to have Frank verify this. Frank still lived in Hong Kong but was traveling in China at the time. I sent him the picture of the crystal skull he had sent me approximately eight years earlier and asked him if this was one of the eight small Himalayan skulls. He wrote back in the affirmative.

One of the other small Himalayan skulls was owned by skull carver Gary "Moonhawk" Butler. Reportedly he polished the skull sometime in 2008 and had the dust from the polishing sent to a lab in Utah to be tested. It's rumored that the tests concluded that this layer was a type of tree sap.[3] That's all we know. Unfortunately, any and all documentation that existed about these skulls was lost when Gary died. (Please see plate 27 of the color insert to view Gary's crystal collection.)

The only way to determine whether these eight skulls are modern or ancient is through scientific testing. You must keep in mind that even if we are able to rule out that modern tools or technology were used to carve them, this would not prove that they are ancient. But if one could rule out any modern tool marks, abrasives, or technology such as lasers or ion probes that may have been used to create them, you have another piece of data or evidence in favor of their ancient origin.

THE STRANGE CASE OF
THE DROPA DISCS

One of the most fascinating aspects of the Himalayan skulls is the claim that odd discs, called Dropa discs, were found with them.

There are many unsubstantiated stories about these Dropa discs. Some people claim that they were inscribed with spiral grooves, which ran from their circumference to their center, like a phonograph record. The claim was also made that there were strange symbols or script in the groves. Some believed that these discs were made by an alien race called the Dropa, who visited Earth thousands of years ago, and that the discs are a kind of information coding or communications device. It was also claimed that they had been found in an ancient cave along with the Himalayan crystal skulls and that hundreds of them had been found. It was rumored that the

Fig. 6.6. Strange stories abound about these mysterious discs, called Dropa discs. Were they made by an alien race called the Dropa, and are they a kind of information coding or communications device?
Photograph courtesy Linda Frisch.

Chinese government subsequently destroyed all the discs for reasons unknown.

The few that survived were supposedly tested by some unnamed Russian scientists and were found to contain some heavy metals like cobalt. It was also reported that they produced a strange-sounding resonance when spun like a record. I tried to track down the source of these stories, and unfortunately they all seem to be fabrications. Russian scientists never studied the discs, and there is no evidence that any science lab researched them. Also, the several known Dropa discs do not have any spiral groves on them, nor are they inscribed with script or symbols.

They resemble the ancient Chinese Pi-discs that were used in funerary rites. Those were usually made of jade. These Dropa discs were of stone, but I also found Pi-discs that had been made of stone, and some of the Dropa discs also appear to have some jade in them. When Frank

Fig. 6.7. Close-up of the surface of a Dropa disc.
Photograph courtesy of Linda Frisch.

Fig. 6.8. Nick Nocerino inspects a Dropa disc. Photograph courtesy of Khrys Nocerino.

Loo brought these Dropa discs to the United States with the Himalayan crystal skulls for the first time, many assumed and believed that these discs were found with the skulls. I recently asked Frank about this, and he explicitly told me that he never said that they had been found together. He also does not believe that there is any relationship between these Dropa discs and the Himalayan skulls and told me this must have been assumed by others.

Nick also told me he didn't believe the Dropa discs and the skulls were of the same origin, and he had not been able to psychically pick up anything from the discs. This was a big disappointment

Fig. 6.9. Linda Frisch's large Himalayan crystal skulls. On the left is Melchezidec, which is the largest of the Himalayan skulls. On the right is White Dove. Both skulls weigh about six pounds and are five inches high; both are composed of quartz crystal. Photograph courtesy of Linda Frisch.

to me, because I had thought this could be an important artifact to study if the discs were, in fact, related in some way to the Himalayan skulls.

Many years ago my good friend Linda Frisch obtained a Dropa disc from Frank. Linda has an incredible collection of crystal skulls and jade artifacts and also owns three original, large Himalayan skulls that she had obtained from Frank Loo.*

Linda is so kind and trustworthy that she offered to mail me her Dropa disc so that I could study and test it in the scanning elec-

---

*Linda administrates a great website, a meeting place for those who own crystal skulls both ancient and modern, and I recommend that you visit the Oracles of Light at http://starelders22.ning.com.

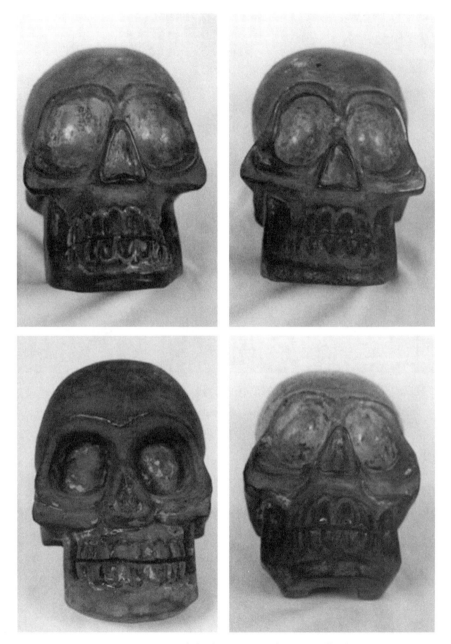

*Fig. 6.10. Four of the large Himalayan skulls that
Frank Loo brought to the United States.
Photograph courtesy of Frank Loo.*

Fig. 6.11. This Himalayan skull was the only one found with an elongated cranium. It is now in the possession of Zane Grant; photograph courtesy of Zane Grant.

tron microscope. Unfortunately, it is too large to fit in the vacuum chamber, and I had to decline the offer. There are few people like Linda, and I appreciated her willingness to risk her own valuable possessions* in the name of science. I hope someday we can do some tests on this disc to determine its composition and possibly how it was produced.

---

*If you're wondering what these skulls and Dropa discs sell for, I was told that their market value is anywhere from hundreds of dollars to three thousand dollars and higher, depending on the size of the skull and its history.

7
Scientific Studies on My Crystal Skulls

I recently obtained a large rock crystal skull from a person who received it from a well-known anthropologist from Argentina who had brought it back from China about fifteen years ago.

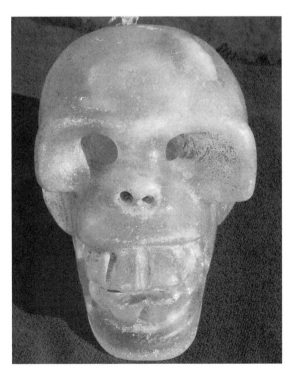

Fig. 7.1. John DeSalvo's ancient crystal skull. Photograph © John DeSalvo.

I wanted to scientifically test both this skull and Hapi, knowing that Hapi was definitely one of the small Himalayan crystal skulls. I decided to test Hapi, my alleged ancient crystal skull, first. With the help of my son Stephen, who is a graduate student in mathematics at the University of Southern California, we found an excellent scanning electron microscope (SEM) testing facility at the University of Minnesota at Duluth, which was only a three-hour drive from where we live. We were specifically looking for a lab that had SEM testing capabilities, which uses a beam of electrons and not light to scan the object. I contacted the lab at UMD and arranged a time for the testing.

METHODOLOGY OF TESTING HAPI

As we have established, a crystal skull is simply a solid piece of quartz crystal that is carved into the shape of a human skull, or at least resembles one in its major characteristics. (The exception is when the jawbone is made separately and later attached, as is the case with the Mitchell-Hedges crystal skull.) Crystal skulls come in a variety of shapes and sizes. What can scientists realistically expect to discover about any of the alleged ancient crystal skulls?

1. It may be possible to determine what part of the world or location the crystal came from (Madagascar or Brazil, for instance), from the physical characteristics of the quartz. We can also determine the type of quartz from which the skull is composed (clear, citrine, or amethyst, for example).
2. Essentially all quartz crystal is hundreds of millions of years old—that's how long it took to form in the veins of the earth.
3. Unfortunately, there are never identification marks on the skull—such as writings, pictures, labels, or hieroglyphs—that could tell us who carved it and when. The carver did not sign his creation like an artist signs their paintings. There are also no ancient documents that reference crystal skulls. We have no

information about how, when, and by whom they were made. (This is analogous to the Great Pyramid of Giza and the Shroud of Turin, two of my major areas of research.)

4. The only other physical information that would be of interest to us is the method by which the crystal skull was carved. Was it carved by hand, with a jeweler's wheel, or with modern equipment? Were any abrasives used to polish it, and were the abrasives ancient or of modern origin? Knowing the answers to these questions helps us to determine if a crystal skull was carved in modern times and/or eliminate it as an ancient one. For example, if we determine that a method was used that was not invented until a certain date or that an abrasive was used that was only produced by a certain date, we know the crystal skull could not be older than that date. This procedure and analysis has allowed us to eliminate three of the candidates of ancient crystal skulls and to reclassify them as modern (the Smithsonian skull, the British Museum skull, and the Paris skull). You will be very surprised when we later discuss another famous crystal skull, which was recently determined to be a modern production.

5. Another thing we could do would be to bombard the skull with all types of electromagnetic energies to see if something happens, or if any changes occur. We could hit it with lasers, ultraviolet light, IR radiation, and/or various particle beams, for instance. Perhaps certain energetic and magnetic fields will cause something to resonate in the quartz structure and it will reveal some information in a new way. I believe these types of experiments need to be done on ancient crystal skulls. As far as I know, this has not been done and I hope to explore this area of research in the future.

I want to state that no crystal skull, as far as I am aware, has undergone testing that has been as scientifically rigorous as mine. It was looked at directly in the SEM in real time and not by making molds or impressions. In addition, energy dispersive spectrometer (EDS) was used to determine the chemical composition of specific surface areas, and this has never before been done on any crystal skulls as far as I know. Also the data was analyzed by scientists and SEM directors at several major universities and not by just one institution. As we will see in the next chapter, the British Museum only viewed the molds of the skulls with the scanning electron microscope because the actual skulls were too large to fit in the vacuum chamber. They also did not do any EDS testing. You have to be able to look at the skull directly in the vacuum chamber to do this. I hoped that SEM/EDS testing could be used to study my crystal skull and possibly determine the carving method.

THE MYSTERY OF THE RED PIGMENT

As mentioned previously, the first time I laid eyes on Hapi, I observed that it had a spotted red coloration all over it. A crystal expert examined it and told me he believed it was an iron oxide patina, which is very common on ancient crystals, especially ones that have been buried. For some reason I had my doubts that it was iron oxide and thought I would like to eventually test this.

In my research about ancient Chinese artifacts I discovered that the ancient Chinese painted many of their ritual objects, especially funerary objects, with a cinnabar paint. Cinnabar is a bright red pigment that was used to make paint in ancient times. The danger with using cinnabar is that it contains mercury, and mercury is very toxic. If you are old enough, you may remember that in the 1950s and 1960s many toys contained mercury. Children's chemistry sets were once sold with liquid mercury. I had one of these when I was a kid. There is a maze toy that contains a drop of mercury, which moves through the maze. Some toys had nonremovable mercury batteries. Who knew at that time that mercury was highly toxic?

I spoke to several curators at well-known museums and universities about cinnabar. There was not too much that they could tell me about it, except that it is definitely toxic and they recommended using rubber latex gloves to handle any object painted with it. To definitively determine what this red pigment was, I would have to do some element testing, which I eventually did. But for now I wanted to know if there was any danger in handling it. I later found an article on the Internet that said cinnabar on ancient artifacts is not toxic, because its mercury would have been depleted over time.

However, I still was not sure, and because of this I decided to check in with a friend of mine, a well-known Egyptologist, author, and college professor, Bob Briar. Professor Briar told me there was no toxicological danger, and I believed him as he spends much time in tombs in Egypt and is one of the most knowledgeable people on this topic. Researching cinnabar gave me the opportunity to become acquainted with a few more curators and make some valuable research connections. No research is a waste of time or a dead end, as you can always learn something and make new friends and colleagues in the process.

THE ACTUAL RESEARCH PROCEDURE

Bryan Bandli is the manager of the lab that carried out the testing on the Himalayan crystal skull given to me by Frank Loo. Bryan is not only a very competent scientist and SEM/EDS technician but also an incredibly nice person who went out of his way to do the tests to my satisfaction and supply me with necessary background information.

The first thing Bryan did was to visually examine the skull and then study it under a stereoscopic light microscope to determine what surface areas of the skull would be the most interesting to look at under the SEM.

After deciding what features we wanted to study closely (the eyes, nose, and teeth), the skull was placed in the SEM vacuum chamber. Because a beam of electrons and not light was being used to scan the image, the sample had to be in a vacuum, or the electrons would strike air molecules and be scattered.

After all the air was pumped out, which took about twenty minutes, we started viewing specific surface areas of the skull. During this time if we wanted to look at a different surface area that was not positioned

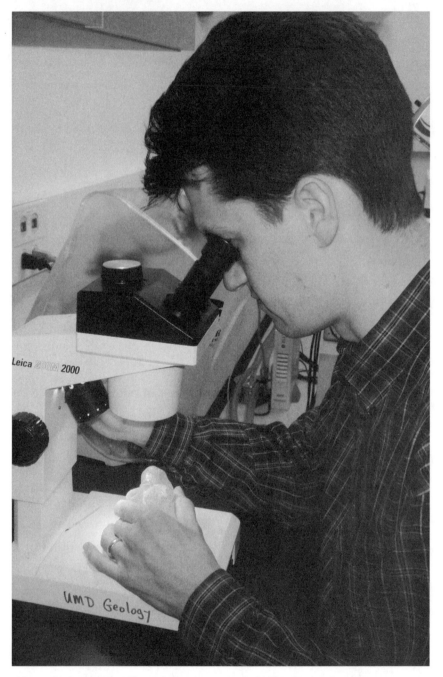

Fig. 7.2. Bryan Bandli studying my crystal skull Hapi under the stereoscopic microscope. Photograph courtesy of Valerie DeSalvo.

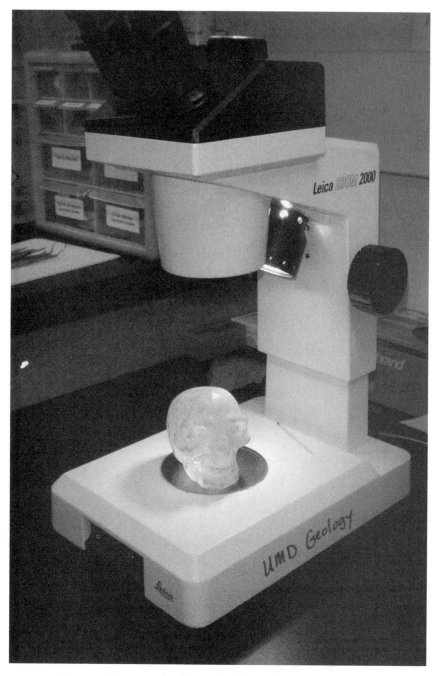

Fig. 7.3. Hapi on display under the stereoscopic microscope.
Photograph courtesy of Valerie DeSalvo.

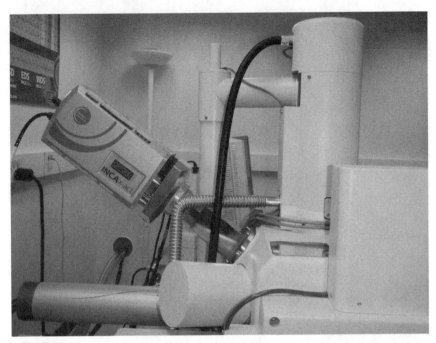

Fig. 7.4. Sophisticated testing equipment such as the scanning electron microscope functioning in conjunction with an EDS unit allows us to take our research further than we've ever dreamed possible. Photograph courtesy of Valerie DeSalvo.

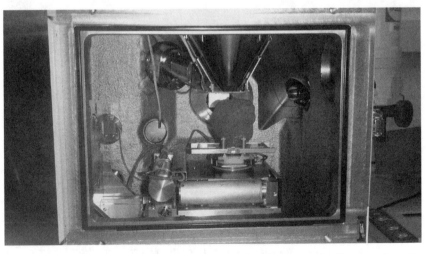

Fig. 7.5. The skull is placed in the vacuum chamber in order for us to be able to view specific areas with the scanning electron microscope. Photograph courtesy of Valerie DeSalvo.

so that it was facing the beam of electrons, we had to open the vacuum chamber and reposition the skull so the new area we wanted to look at was pointing up.

Then the air was again pumped out. The image was displayed on a large computer screen, and because we were looking at the skull in real time we could scan the beam across the surface until we found an area of interest that we wanted to study in detail and with increased magnification. What an advantage to this procedure in contrast to the British Museum study, in which they were limited by having to make molds or impressions and could only view those.

Fig. 7.6. We pinpoint an area of interest on the surface of my crystal skull. Photograph courtesy of Valerie DeSalvo.

What's so amazing about this type of scanning electron microscopy is that it also has an EDS unit attached to it, which allows an analysis of the atomic composition of the surface under examination. The chemical composition (i.e., the specific elements present in that area, for example iron, nitrogen, potassium, etc.) of that area is displayed on a large computer monitor to the right of the one showing the SEM image. Each peak is a specific element, and its height is its relative amount or concentration.

SCIENTIFIC ANALYSIS OF HAPI

When the tests were completed I decided to send the SEM/EDS data to a number of SEM directors and geologists at several universities in the United States and Canada for analysis. It is always best to get as many expert opinions as possible and see where they agree or disagree. Here are their conclusions.

1. Every expert who looked at the SEM scans could not find any indication of rotary wheels, lasers, ion probe marks, or strong acid application. Thus there is *no* evidence that Hapi is a modern production or a forgery. This does not necessarily prove it is ancient.

2. Several experts believe that a large part of the surface area evidenced a very slow acidic etching, which may have been caused by running water or weak acids. They speculated that this etching could be the result of the skull having been buried in the ground for long periods of time—hundreds or thousands of years in my estimation—where it was affected by humeric acid in the soil. Because humeric acid in the soil is very weak, the process would indeed take an extremely long time.

   The surface of the skull does not show any evidence of fast acid etching, such as would be the case if a strong acid like hydrofluoric acid had been employed. Evidence of a fast-acting acid would point to a modern application. However, there is no evidence of an application by strong acids; the SEM scans would have revealed that.

3. What is very interesting is that in the eye socket area there is no indication of acid etching but evidence of primitive hand tooling, which would be consistent with it being an ancient production. Because the eye sockets are very well rounded, it is possible that they originally could have held a stone or gem. Or maybe the eyes were painted, as seen in some ancient jade skulls from China, which would explain the absence of acid etching in this area. This is merely speculation.

4. Finally, the energy dispersive spectroscopy data shows the presence of a thin hydrocarbon coating on some areas on the surface of the skull. This is consistent with what I was told by Frank Loo and others about tests done on a similar Himalayan skull that also had this red coating. As mentioned earlier, Gary Butler brought some of the coating from one of these other small Himalayan skulls to the University of Utah to be tested many years ago, and the coating was shown to be a tree resin. (Please see plate 27 of the color insert for Gary Butler's crystal collection.)

There are stories that the ancient Tibetans would coat their spiritual artifacts with a resin before they buried them to retain the psychic or spiritual energy. If indeed this coating is tree resin, this may possibly lend itself to carbon-14 dating as tree resin is carbon based. Maybe this date would tell us when the skull was actually coated with this resin and give us some idea of its age.

One interesting point is that the number of teeth carved into my crystal skull is about sixteen, perhaps eighteen (it's difficult to make out the lines exactly). Nick Nocerino once told Frank Loo a secret many years ago. According to Nick, all ancient skulls have less than twenty-four teeth.

Fig. 7.7. Gary "MoonHawk" Butler at the Garden of the Gods in Colorado
Springs, Colorado, with his carving of the "Blue Star Maiden."
Photograph courtesy of Lynn Johnson.

THE PSYCHIC ANALYSIS OF HAPI

In the following discussion I would like to address the results of studies I did with four psychics: Becky Andreasson, Helene Olsen, Ann Hall, and Richard Shafsky, a crystal skull expert with psychic abilities. (See Richard's incredible experience with the Mayan crystal skull in the appendix.) I asked them to do psychometry on my crystal skull before they knew any of the results of the scientific testing.

Becky Andreasson

Becky told me that Hapi is a very ancient crystal skull from the Tibetan Chinese area and that its energy is strong and powerful. She felt the energy coming from the eyes to be especially powerful. She believes that there may be alien energy associated with it and also felt that the skull was a kind of transmitter or communications device.

Helene Olsen

Helene's psychic information was incredibly similar, but she added a very interesting piece of information. Helene also believed it was from Tibet and very ancient, possibly thousands or tens of thousands of years old. She also sensed extreme energy associated with the skull and that it shot out rays from the eyes. She felt it was a strange energy, nothing she had ever experienced, and felt that it might be associated with aliens in some way. She was very moved to have been asked to work with it and felt honored by its powerful and different energy. Helene was convinced, and I cannot emphasize this strongly enough, that the skull is a transmitter. A transmitter to what she could not say, but she felt it had a tremendous potential if its secrets could be unlocked. She felt psychically connected to Hapi and received the following information psychically.

> The skull referred to himself as Dropa. I feel this entity connected to my own thoughts in that I previously heard the possible name

of his culture. The beings of this culture are small and diminutive, with large flat faces. Their eyes are quite round and large, with a dark iris, which is quite in contrast to their pale body. Their body is translucent with a slightly pink-gray cast to their "skin." They are wearing sheaths or a type of lightweight clothing that resembles robes. Their physical bodies do not feel "meaty." They have a very heavy energy body around them, which supports their physical body. They do not communicate verbally with each other often, and they are extremely quiet in movement. They are cave dwellers and prefer dawn and twilight times.

These beings are "chemical intuitives" in that they are able to figure out the interactions of naturally occurring chemicals and compounds. They also know the interactions of compounds and how these compounds can interact with the energetic and physical body.

Hapi describes their "etching" of stone as "easy." In my third-eye vision I was able to view details of the process that they used to "etch" the skull. He showed me a small flexible twig with a bunch of small yellow "berries" on it, which he referred to as "fruit seed pods." No animal eats these because they are too caustic. These berries are mashed with a very thin two- to three-inch-long pointy leaf. Then a thick, dark green leaf is cut out in the shape they want to "carve." They use the cutout leaf design like a pattern and then spread the paste on it. The pattern with the paste on it is then placed precisely where they require the "etching." The object is then placed on a flat, heat-absorbent rock in full sun.

A "tripod" with a crystal (I think; possibly it is a water bubble) is placed over the carving area to magnify the sunlight on this pasted leaf. Then the object is checked after two days of full sun. All of the debris is cleaned off, and the same process is repeated by placing the pattern and paste on once again. There are many natural compounds that make this acid, and this was a typical way of "carving" in that culture at that time. The skulls were carved in the Dropa image because they were used for communication and for healing in that culture. I thought the Dropa interacted with the local natives in China, but they really did not to any large extent.

During this reading I didn't get any information about where they came from, but I was able to determine that they were from China (Tibet), Atlantis, Egypt (early on), and India before recorded history and before the . . . Egyptian cultures were known by us.

It's important to realize that Helene told me all this without her knowing the results of the scientific testing.[1]

Ann Hall

As a scientist, the more data you can accumulate, the more valid your conclusion. Thus, I decided to get another psychometric analysis of my crystal skull. I had just recently started working with Ann Hall in her capacity as a psychic medium, but I had known her as a friend for some time. What I admire most about her is that she does pro bono psychic work for local law enforcement investigators in their search for missing persons. Ann lives in Maine, and, like Becky and Helene, she is very gifted.

It is interesting that Ann uses crystals in all her psychic work, whether to do a reading or while working on a criminal case. (Please see plate 28 of the color insert to view Ann's crystal collection.) She told me, "When I practice map dowsing on a missing person's case, I use a pendulum; I have been assigned a spirit guide for that pendulum. For great focus and alignment I choose the crystal ball. For celestial help and a calming effect I choose fluorite. The calcite shows me many layers of a situation and allows me to project myself out of my body. The selenite wand brings out my spiritual side more clearly. The blue angelite sphere helps me connect more deeply to the angelic realm, and the quartz crystal brings me excellent clarity on situations."[2]

After doing some psychometry work with Ann, I told her that what she needed to do was to make some observation or prediction that later could be validated. Several days later she sent me an e-mail. It is the only prediction she has ever made to me so it is not that she is predicting things every day and one prediction happens to turn out to be correct. I received the following e-mail from Ann on February 3, 2011.

> John, This is most unusual. The other day during Enochian meditation I was finishing up and I felt compelled to say out loud: Suleiman. I didn't know that this was the name of the Vice President of Egypt! I just found that out by watching ABC News this evening. I have a feeling Mr. Suleiman is going to be killed. That's between you and me for now. Also it will be soon. Ann

Well, you could not give a more specific prediction! She mentioned a specific name (Suleiman), a specific event (an assassination), and a specific time ("soon"). After reading the e-mail I forgot about it. Several days later I heard that there was an attempted assassination on Omar Suleiman, the Vice President of Egypt. I checked the Internet, and it was all over the news media. According to the story, the attempted assassination failed, but it left two of his bodyguards dead. The Egyptian government denied this assassination attempt, but many people believe it was for real. The news report came out on February 5, two days after Ann had made this prediction.

I don't know about you, but one prediction with incredible specifics is very impressive for a psychic, in my opinion. That the assassination attempt was not successful was not important. Predictions do not always come out 100 percent as there are random events and free will that change the outcome. Thus, I wanted to include Ann's psychic impressions on my crystal skull. Again, she did not have much information about it except it was a crystal skull that I was researching.

I will summarize what she said.

She told me that when I meditate I should also massage the temples of the skull as this would allow me to tap in to it. She said that she saw stone walls all around the skull and felt like it was in a cave. She saw other caves and also stalactites that were associated with the skull. The people that carved it were diminutive and were in a trance at the time of its carving. A glacial ice shift was present at the time of the carving, and the skull would be buried in the sand when it was not in use. It benefited from being in the moonlight, especially the full moon. She also told me that an archangel was and is involved with this skull.

I thought this was very consistent with what Becky and Helene had said and also what the research showed. She mentioned it was buried in the sand when it was not being used, which would be consistent with the evidence of humeric acid etching that had been detected previously. She was consistent with the other psychics in that in her vision the people that carved it were from antiquity and were quite small. That it was in a cave is consistent with legends about these skulls.

Richard Shafsky

The last person to do psychic research on Hapi was Richard Shafsky, but before I discuss that I would like to go into how my connection to him came about. I thought it would be a great idea if I asked my very close friend Khrys Nocerino, the wife of the late Nick Nocerino, if I could interview her for my book. Because Nick had been my mentor, my very close and dear friend, and the world's greatest crystal skull expert, it seemed very appropriate to include an interview with his widow in this book.

I believed this would be an opportunity for Khrys to talk about Nick and his work, but when I asked her, she was reluctant. However, she told me about a person who was good friends with Nick, who had traveled with him on his expeditions to Mexico. She suggested I speak with him and told me that his name was Richard Shafsky. The name sounded familiar, but I couldn't place it. Khrys went on to tell me that he had recently contacted her and told her that he wanted to get in touch with me, so she had given him my phone number.

I was very excited because I believed that Richard might be able to shed some interesting light on ShaNaRa, including stories about the initial expedition in which Nick discovered ShaNaRa. More to the point, I wanted to meet someone who had been as close to Nick as I was. Khrys gave me Richard's number and I called him right away. I got him on the first ring, and after speaking with him for almost an hour I was transfixed when I got off the phone.

Not only had Richard been with Nick and traveled with him in Mexico, but Richard was the person who had actually brought the famous Mayan crystal skull to the United States with another person and was its caretaker for a period of time. (That's probably why his name was familiar to me.) (See Richard's story of this in the appendix.) He too was very excited about our contact.* I asked him if he would like to contribute to my book, and he said he would be happy to do so. He also graciously agreed to do a reading of my ancient crystal skull Hapi.

According to Richard, my crystal skull was carved about 10,000 to 12,000 years ago somewhere in or near Tibet at a time when the ice age was ending. *Homo sapiens* were running the risk of becoming extinct, and we needed a lot of help. Aliens appeared on Earth; some of them were helpful and others not so much. My crystal skull was carved by humans but under the direction or guidance of aliens. Humans were not really working with crystals at that time, so that's why alien guidance was needed. These aliens were not that genetically different from us, and that's why the skull looks human but is slightly different. Hapi actually does look like early man. Richard knew of three other skulls like Hapi, all baseball size, and also believed that the location of one of these is in the Vatican.

My skull is more of a receiver than anything else. Information sent by the aliens would have been received by the human who possessed the

---

*What I was most touched about was that Richard told me that before Nick died, he had told him that I was the one person he could trust. This was one of the nicest compliments I have ever had. I am honored and very grateful to Richard for contributing information about my crystal skull to this book.

skull. It was also used as a tracking device for the human who possessed it. It was not made for worship or idolatry but for information storage. Richard went on to say that my skull was jam-packed with information and we would have to do certain things to make this information accessible. Even though we have no absolute proof this crystal skull is ancient (unless we carbon date the resin), all the evidence points to it being an ancient crystal skull, thousands of years old.

Please keep in mind that *none* of the alleged ancient crystal skulls, famous or not, has ever been subjected to the testing that mine has. All evidence points to my crystal skull as not being a modern production. Instead, all indications point to it being an ancient crystal skull.

BACKGROUND ON ANOTHER CRYSTAL SKULL

As mentioned at the beginning of this chapter, a life-size, seven-pound rock crystal skull recently came into my possession. It was brought to the United States from China about fifteen years ago by an anthropologist from Argentina and eventually came into my possession from a friend of his. He had recently passed away. There is, however, no documented provenance of this skull, and this information is just word of mouth. The anthropologist believed it was from the Hongshan culture of ancient China.

The Hongshan culture flourished in northeast China from around 5000 to 3000 BCE, making it 5,000 to 7,000 years old. This period is classified as the late Neolithic period, also known as the last part of the Stone Age. The Hongshan archaeological site was discovered by a Japanese archaeologist in 1908 and excavated in 1935. Numerous burial artifacts made of jade were found, as well as some small copper rings. These people did extensive work in jade, creating everything from everyday utensils to religious amulets and everything in between. They also worked with stone and clay.

An underground temple complex was also discovered at the Hongshan archaeological site along with an altar and clay female heads, which possibly represent deities. In fact, there is some evidence that this culture may have been the first to use feng shui due to the discovery of round and square shapes representing heaven and Earth. (Early feng shui was based on astronomy and its relationship to the Earth.) Several small jade skulls were also found at this site, but crystal skulls and crystal ornaments from this period are not very common.

METHODOLOGY OF TESTING
A LARGE ANCIENT CRYSTAL SKULL

I brought this large rock crystal skull to geologist Scott Wolter in St. Paul, Minnesota, for testing. Scott has authored eight books and has been president of American Petrographic Services since 1990 where he manages the independent petrographic analysis testing laboratory. This lab is also where the Kensington Rune Stone was tested in 2000. He's been the principal petrographer in more than five thousand investigations throughout the United States and around the world, including the evaluation of fire-damaged concrete at the Pentagon following the attacks of September 11, 2001. Scott agreed to examine my crystal skull using a digital computerized microscope system. This is state-of-the-art and very advanced technology, superior in certain ways to the scanning electron microscope. This computerized microscope system is so fascinating in that Scott was able to scan a specific area of the skull, at increasing and decreasing degrees of focus. The computer would then construct a three-dimensional image of that area. This is like looking right into the markings on the skull. We could also color-code the depth of various areas of the skull and even rotate it in any direction. It is incredible what is revealed by this technique.

During several intense hours of study, Scott generated many scans of different, carved areas of the skull (see images above as well as plate 29 of the color insert). We were looking for signs that modern equipment and technology had been employed in its creation. We were also attempting to ascertain how the carving had been done. At the end of the testing, Scott concluded that he could not identify any modern tool marks or evidence that any modern equipment had been used in its production. It appears to have been carved by hand using primitive methods. The weathering pattern is also consistent with it being very old. Although he could not give me a definite age, he personally felt it was ancient and a very rare archaeological artifact.

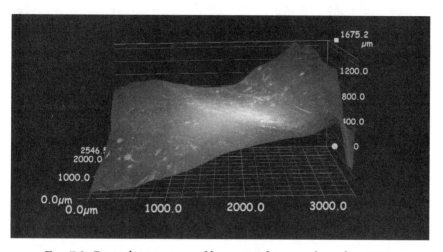

Fig. 7.8. Digital microscopy of lower top front tooth surface 100X.
Photograph courtesy of Scott Wolter.

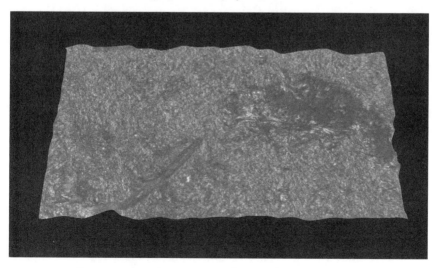

Fig. 7.9. Digital microscopy of upper lip surface 400X.
Photograph courtesy of Scott Wolter.

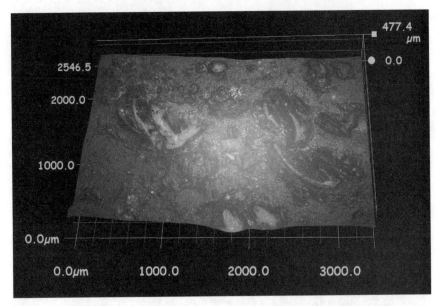

*Fig. 7.10. Digital microscopy of top skull surface 100X.
Photograph courtesy of Scott Wolter.*

I was very excited to think about all the famous skulls that had been tested and turned out to be fake, whereas mine might be an authentic ancient crystal skull thousands of years old. Perhaps one day additional testing will be done on this skull, but in the meantime I believe the evidence overwhelmingly points to this being an authentic life-size ancient crystal skull.

PSYCHIC ANALYSIS OF A
LARGE ANCIENT CRYSTAL SKULL

Here are the results of the psychometry on this crystal skull by the psychometrists I work with.

Becky Andreasson
It does feel old . . . and I sense an alien connection too. I feel the presence of sulfur also, which is strange! It doesn't really feel negative, but it does feel very different from the other crystal skulls! It has a different

vibration coming from it, which is rough and primitive—a bulky feeling, which is kind of strange. Maybe it has something to do with the Yeti* culture of old!

Helene Olsen

Helene told me she felt that the skull was approximately five thousand years old, making it consistent with the Hongshan culture. She also said it had a strange and primitive energy, which was very different from what she had experienced from archaeological objects in the past. She also felt there was an alien component, or that aliens had been involved in its production. She went on to say that she believes that humans had actually carved it but had been directed by the aliens. She also said it was a storage device for information and possibly a transmitter or receiver as well.

Richard Shafsky

Richard believed that it had been made by humans but under the direction of aliens, like my smaller, baseball-size crystal skull. According to him the skull is approximately five thousand years old and originated in China.

It's also a receiver like the small one and jammed with information, the difference between the two skulls being that the small Himalayan crystal skull was produced by a different group of aliens. The aliens involved with the large crystal skull are mysterious, and he couldn't tell me too much about them except for the fact that they have not appeared on Earth for thousands of years, nor had they been in any kind of contact with our planet for that same amount of time. In our distant past they were present in Central America and many parts of Asia. He doesn't know where they are from or what they want; however, he doesn't think they are evil. It's possible, according to him, that they are interdimensional.

---

*The Yeti, or Abominable Snowman, is an unidentified ape-like creature that has allegedly inhabited the Himalayas since antiquity. The legend of the Yeti is a pre-Buddhist belief, which posits that the people of ancient Nepal and Tibet worshipped a glacial being.

CONCLUSIONS

In conclusion what do I, John DeSalvo, think of this large ancient crystal skull? The short time I have spent with this crystal skull has convinced me that it is a real ancient crystal skull thousands of years old. I also believe it is somehow connected with some ancient culture or beings we have not heard of. What these are I cannot say. They may be aliens, multidimensional beings, time travelers, or a lost or ancient culture. I have no idea and cannot speculate. I do feel the presence of something with this skull but cannot identify what it is. I am honored that it came into my hands, and I will always take good care of it.

8
Other Research and Results of Scientific Tests on Alleged Ancient Crystal Skulls

Now we will look specifically at the results of testing done on crystal skulls by the British Museum, Hewlett-Packard, some laboratories in France, and Bell Labs.

THE BRITISH MUSEUM TESTS

In 1996 the British Museum decided to take part in the testing of certain alleged ancient crystal skulls. Four of the famous ancient crystal skulls were tested: ShaNaRa (owned by Nick Nocerino), Max (owned by JoAnn Parks), the British Museum skull, and the Smithsonian crystal skull. Several other skulls not as well known were also tested. Both JoAnn and her husband, Carl, as well as Nick, had flown to London for these tests. Because all of these skulls were too large to fit into the vacuum chamber of the SEM, molds or impressions had to be made of smaller surface areas. After the tests were completed, everyone waited in suspense for the results; however, the British Museum declined to release the results of the tests that were done on Max and ShaNaRa, adding that it was their policy not to do any tests on privately owned artifacts. Why did the museum agree to these tests if they weren't going to release the results?

Some people have speculated that the tests may not have been conducted, but Nick and JoAnn said that they personally saw the staff make plastic molds of both ShaNaRa and Max, and thus they believe that the testing was done. Others believe that the tests may have revealed the presence of modern tooling or abrasives and the museum was afraid of potential litigation because the owners made money with their skulls. This argument doesn't really make sense, though, because Nick and JoAnn had signed written affidavits in which they agreed not to argue with the museum's results and never to take any legal action against it.

Others speculate that the museum found evidence of ancient technology or something that could not be explained and didn't want to release the test results for that reason. The salient point here is that these tests can be done anywhere, even at the lab that I used for my SEM tests, and, given this, I hope that in the near future JoAnn Parks and Khrys Nocerino will allow further testing of their crystal skulls.

I personally believe that the decision made by the British Museum was wrong. Science should be open and research information not withheld. I hope someday they decide to make their discoveries known to the public.

Findings on the British Museum Crystal Skull and the Smithsonian Crystal Skull

The museum was able to determine that the British Museum crystal skull was made with modern tools and the carving dates to the nineteenth century. The Smithsonian crystal skull was also found to be a modern carving. The researchers at the museum discovered it had been carved using a substance known as carborundum, a modern abrasive. They also believe it was carved within the past one hundred years. These findings were published, but because the results are highly technical, I won't bore you with the details here. Instead I will refer you to a definitive article titled "The Origins of Two Purportedly Pre-Columbian Mexican Crystal Skulls," which discusses them.[1]

HEWLETT-PACKARD TESTS OF THE MITCHELL-HEDGES SKULL

When this skull first surfaced in 1933 there were questions about its authenticity. Later, auction records were found, feeding the theory that Mitchell-Hedges had indeed acquired it at a public sale, but these records were soon forgotten. Frank Dorland, a well-known art conservator and collector, had been in possession of the Mitchell-Hedges skull since the mid-1960s. Frank worked as a consultant to many of the top museums in the United States, and it was Frank who, in the early 1970s, brought the skull to the labs for testing after Anna Mitchell-Hedges gave him permission to do so.

The Hewlett-Packard Company, founded in 1935, specializes in manufacturing computers, storage devices, networking hardware, oscillators, software, and all kinds of electronic devices. The tests were carried out at their laboratories in Santa Clara, California.

Scientific Analysis and Assessment
The tests initially determined that the Mitchell-Hedges crystal skull was indeed clear and made of very pure quartz crystal that had formed naturally within the earth. There are several tests that can determine this, and the one that was employed was one in which the skull was immersed in a container of benzyl alcohol, a colorless organic liquid whose formula is $C_6H_5CH_2OH$. Benzyl

alcohol has the same refractive index* and density as quartz crystal.

If the object was really quartz, when placed in this solution it would blend in with the solution and literally disappear. This would prove that they have the same refractive index and verify that the object is made from quartz. This was the case with the Mitchell-Hedges crystal skull. A second way to verify that it's quartz is to shine a polarized light into it. If veils are seen inside, the substance indeed is quartz. I have done this many times.

The Mitchell-Hedges crystal skull is different from the other alleged ancient crystal skulls in that it has a detachable jaw, whereas the other skulls are carved from one piece of crystal. The question then becomes: Was the jaw made from the same piece of crystal as the main skull? In this case the answer was yes, and I surmise that the original piece of crystal must have been very large to be able to produce both these pieces.

The Mitchell-Hedges skull was also studied under the microscope at high magnification (this was not, however, an electron microscope, which would have revealed much more detail), and no evidence of modern tooling or use of modern equipment to carve the image was found. This led the researchers to believe that the skull had been carved by hand, employing a simple carving technique. They could not determine how it was carved or when, but they did rule out evidence of modern equipment. Some speculated that it was produced slowly by rubbing the crystal with sand, diamond grains, and water over a long period of time. How long? No one could say for sure, but one scientist speculated it would have taken a minimum of three hundred years.

Optic experiments were also performed on the skull, which determined that the skull would channel light in a specific way. If, for example, a light was placed below the skull and made to shine upward, the light would emerge out of the eyes. A special technique would

---

*The refractive index is the measure of the speed of light in that medium.

have been employed in the carving to ensure this effect. This reveals to us the incredible craftsmanship that went in to the carving of this skull.

The researchers also were able to demonstrate that the skull had been carved against its normal or natural axis of formation. This was a difficult task because typically when this is done the crystal will shatter and fracture, but it can be done by a good carver. Most carvers only carve in the natural axis of the mineral. At the time this testing was done in the early 1970s, the conclusions about this skull were as follows: it was natural quartz crystal; there was no evidence that it was a modern creation; it was an object that had been made with extreme precision; and it had light-reflecting properties. Its age could not be conclusively determined, nor could it be determined how it had been carved.

LATER TESTS ON
THE MITCHELL-HEDGES
SKULL BY THE SMITHSONIAN MUSEUM

Even today many people do not know of special tests done on this skull by the Smithsonian Museum of Natural History in 2008 conducted by Jane Walsh. While they may know of the British Museum tests done in the 1990s on the Smithsonian and British Museum skulls, they may have never heard of this later one on the Mitchell-Hedges crystal skull.

In 2008 the Mitchell-Hedges skull was brought to the Smithsonian Museum by its caretaker, Bill Homann, who had become its caretaker upon Anna Mitchell-Hedges' death in 2007. At the museum it would be filmed for a Smithsonian Network documentary titled *Legend of the Crystal Skull*.

Scientific Analysis and Assessment
Smithsonian anthropologist Jane Walsh decided to examine the skull's surface tool marks using a scanning electron microscope.

Because the skull was too large to fit in the vacuum chamber, molds or impressions were made in what we now know to be standard operating procedure.

The micrographs of the Mitchell-Hedges skull, according to Walsh, showed evidence of the use of a high-speed cutting or carving tool. Some of these carved lines are less than a millimeter thick, which indicates that a steel or iron tool was used to carve the lines. There was also evidence that wheeled tools—not available to the pre-Columbians—were employed. Walsh thus concluded that this skull was carved in modern times using a high-speed, diamond-coated, rotary cutting tool of a very small size. She believes this is twentieth-century technology, which would be consistent with records indicating that the skull initially surfaced in 1933.[2] I have studied the micrographs and I agree 100 percent with her findings.

FRENCH TESTS ON THE PARIS CRYSTAL SKULL

It's interesting that there were some scientific studies done by a French lab* on an alleged ancient crystal skull known as the Paris crystal skull in 2007 and 2008. This crystal skull, made from very clear quartz, is about four inches high, weighs about six pounds, and has a hole drilled through its center. It's housed in the Musee du Quai Branly in Paris and is thought to be of pre-Columbian origin. There is no real documented provenance of this skull except it initially appeared in the museum collection in the late nineteenth century.

Scientific Analysis and Assessment

After testing was done on the Paris crystal skull, scientists concluded that it was not ancient and certainly not pre-Columbian. Modern tool marks were discovered, along with marks that evidenced the use of modern abrasives. In fact, by testing pockets of water sealed in the crys-

---

*The Center for Research and Restoration of the Museums in France

tal, they could date the skull to the nineteenth century. They actually studied it again in 2009 using scanning electron microscopy and confirmed their findings.

BELL LABS AND HEWLETT-PACKARD TESTS ON THE MAYAN CRYSTAL SKULL

The Mayan crystal skull was studied both at Hewlett-Packard and Bell Labs. It was brought there for tests by Nick Nocerino and Richard Shafsky. The story of how it eventually arrived in the United States from Mexico is told by Richard Shafsky in the appendix.

Scientific Analysis and Assessment
Here is Richard's account of the testing that was done on the Mayan crystal skull.

After Nick and I brought the Mayan crystal skull back from Mexico safely, we decided to subject it to tests at Bell Labs and Hewlett Packard. These tests would be done employing different variables of light, piezoelectric effects, sound, and color. One result of these tests was the attainment of its precise weight and measurements. We also discovered that it had no surface marks of any kind, which would indicate how it was formed. Because the skull was so large that we couldn't use an electron microscope on it, we used high-powered light and dark field microscopes instead.

The crystal skull was formed all the way against the axis of the stone, which should have caused shattering. When subjected to monochromatic and laser light of various colors, the skull emanated different scenes. The scientists were downright dumfounded. The skull went through spectral and internal visual changes with various tones and notes, as well as with color. For instance, using a synthesizer and hitting the note middle C could open a landscape; hitting F-sharp would open another scene. While playing a scale at whatever tempo was selected, the scenes would alter and continue changing with each note and shift in tempo variation.

While exposing the skull to different, colored beams of light, it reacted in a similar fashion. Targeting any point on the head produced another result, which indicated without a shadow of a doubt that every minute particle of the skull contained memory, records, or access to records. If a colored beam was placed on one of its teeth, a light would emanate out of the head or the temple at an unpredictable point and new scenes would be displayed internally. Piezo-electric tests were also applied. Padded mounts on a vise applied pressure around the skull at various points. Depending on where the pressure was applied, scenes were activated within the skull.

Sometimes one of the eye sockets was "closed" off from activity at which point we hooked up the skull with sensors, as if we were conducting an EEG. There were measurable oscillations in high frequency ranges, indicating activity. They were not like brain activity patterns any of us had seen, but there was a measurable activity, not unlike electricity, with corresponding spikes and changes that occurred when different scenes were revealed. The skull also emanated light, indicating an internal power source, just as the EEG had indicated brain or energy wavelengths. We could not determine if the power source came from within or if it was external.

An infrared camera was used to take photos of the entire process.

When Nick and I left the labs we left behind a group of bewildered scientists. We didn't share with them what we already knew to be true: the skull is a quantum tool and a portal. It allows access to other dimensions, time, and space. We do not know how it operates. We do not know who made it. We do not know its exact origin. We do not know how it records. But those of us who had the privilege to interact with the Mayan skull have had our minds and consciousness opened in a way that defies explanation.

Nick and I were both able to witness this remarkable object,

*Fig. 8.1. Infrared photo of Mayan crystal skull taken
at the Hewlett-Packard lab in 1979.
Copyright © Richard Shafsky.*

which inspires and intrigues everyone who comes into contact with it. It holds our records but does not determine our future. Where it is today we do not know; we only know that wherever it is, it is still recording its surroundings while at the same time emanating energy and light.

PART THREE

─── ✳ ───

Scrying, Meditating, and Magical Rituals

9
Scrying with Crystals

Most people believe that scrying is done with a crystal ball, yet it can also refer to seeing psychic visions in crystals, mirrors, water, smoke, clouds, and numerous other types of materials. The visions seen by the scryer (the person looking into the crystal ball) can be from the past, present, or future (which is known as divination). It may not always be apparent to the scryer which one of these timeframes the vision is from. Some people claim to be able to see visions of higher spiritual realms or the heavens and/or unknown alien worlds.

THE THEORY BEHIND SCRYING

I would like to explain how I believe scrying works and the theory behind it by using the following illustration. Let's imagine that you are sitting in a moving train and its forward movement represents actual time moving forward. You must remain in your seat and thus can only look out the window to see what's happening in your present time. All of a sudden a hatch opens in the roof of the train and you get on a ladder and climb up. You then can put your head through the hatch and look out from the top of the train. If you happen to be looking forward in the direction the train is traveling, you'll see things up ahead in the future before the train reaches them. If you happen to be facing toward the back of the train, as you stick your head out of the hatch, you would see things that the train has passed—in other words, the past.

If you are looking to your left or right, that is in the present time, you can only see things in the present, but you can see much farther away than when you were inside the train just looking out one of the windows. In fact, you can see far into the distance because you are up high. You can also then see things happening in the present time that you could not see when you were inside the train. Maybe you could see things happening in different lands (this is an example of how remote viewing may work).

Thus, by being on top of the train and being able to look to the front, the back, or the sides, you can now see things from the past, the future, and far away—things that you couldn't see while confined to your seat inside the train. You may only be able to see one and not all of these views; in other words, only the past, the present, or the future. It depends on the gift or ability of the scryer whether they can see one or more of these views. This analogy can also be applied to other techniques of clairvoyance, telepathy, divination, and psychic development. Suffice it to say that this may give us some idea how the mechanism of scrying works.

Unfortunately, when you mention crystal balls and scrying to most people they immediately associate someone trying to see in to the future. Divination, or seeing in to the future, is only one aspect of scrying, as we discussed. I would like to take my analogy further and say that if they looked upward toward the sky you might be able to see other higher dimensions and alien worlds. (One of the reasons that, in recent years, I have been drawn again to quartz crystal, and especially crystal balls, is because of their use in ritual magic and their utility when used to see in to the spiritual world.) The view one happens to have depends on one's gifts, and perhaps pure chance also. It's possible that some people may have the ability to control what direction they can look toward. Thus, in our analogy, they may be able to turn around on top of the ladder and see in any direction they choose, and even look upward. Only with practice and experience can you determine where your talent lies as you develop the ability to see into many, if not all, of these directions.

PRACTICE MAKES PERFECT

I have practiced and experimented with scrying for many years and don't feel I have any special talent or gift in this area. Admittedly, at times I have seen things that I believe were psychic visions, but these didn't come frequently or easily to me. I seem to have the best results when I am in a deep meditative state—an altered state of consciousness. Due to the fact that, over time, I was seeing better and more consistent results, I came to the realization that with enough practice, anyone can eventually attain tangible results.

If, after much practice and persistence over a long period of time, you still are unsuccessful, maybe it would be better to move on to something else that you have more of a natural ability for. For example, I am a terrible singer and no matter how much practice or how many lessons I may have, I still cannot sing a song in key. But since childhood, I was a very talented drummer with a natural-born ability. Thus I believe that we need to identify where our natural abilities and talents lie and focus on those. My natural abilities lie in the field of magic, however, I only found that out after thirty years of spiritual searching.

I'm assuming you want to try your luck with scrying, so that's why I've written this chapter. In it I will give you valuable suggestions, which I have accumulated over the years, from excellent sources. I hope my suggestions help you and you have success with your endeavors. It's worth a shot! The key word is *perseverance*!

I want to discuss something that is quite important in the area of psychic development. A good friend of mine who has had a lot of experience with scrying told me that it doesn't matter whether you scry into a beautiful quartz crystal ball, or just use some ink in a bowl of water, or just look at the clouds. The crystal ball, water, or clouds are just tools to open your psychic center. They are, in a sense, a catalyst. If you remember from your chemistry class, a catalyst is something that speeds up a chemical reaction but is not involved in it and is not affected by it. That is what these objects (crystal ball, water, or clouds) are. Some people may have better results with quartz than other substances. Some may prefer obsidian or black mirrors, or even use clouds as a scrying tool. It's an individual preference, and whatever works for you, use it. I discovered that black mirrors work better for me than crystal balls. You just have to experiment and try different things.

You might be interested to know that the ancients used an incredible variety of objects for scrying, including crystals, mirrors, water with dye, polished steel, liquid poured into the palm of their hands, a drop of blood, the blade of a sword, and even a human fingernail. I'm sure you could come up with other objects that would also work. A very interesting example comes from India, where ashes are used, or incense moistened with castor oil, which is then poured into the palm of the scryer's hand. Some spiritualists from the late nineteenth and early twentieth centuries used a variety of gems and jewelry, and even the surface of a polished table. Many scryers, both past and present, believe that even though all of these types of materials and objects can be used for scrying, quartz crystal, for some reason, is the best.

As stated elsewhere in this book, I believe that quartz crystal has an important property in that it holds psychic information and is a psychic transmitter. It's a matrix connecting crystals throughout the world, the universe, and other dimensions. In addition to helping us to see visions of the past, present, future, and other realms, I believe it can help us with something even more important, that is, information concerning our own selves. It can help us to open insights into our soul, our natural and spiritual abilities, and most importantly, our spiritual path.

This is very important because many of us go through life not really identifying our weaknesses or our strengths. If we honestly identified these and worked on our weaknesses and maximized our strengths, I believe we would be more successful and happier in life.

Also, we are all on a spiritual path and if crystals can help us discern this path and guide us as we proceed along it, what a wonderful benefit this would be.

SCRYING TIPS

Here are some tips I've collected over the many years of experimenting; I believe they may be very useful to you. You will be given more details for meditating with crystals in a future chapter, but this general information about scrying will hopefully help you succeed with the meditation technique.

First, you need to be in the proper state of mind and attitude to succeed with scrying. I would suggest you do it in the evening or early morning when there may be more of a quiet time in your environment. This is just a general suggestion; it's up to you to decide on the best time to do it.

Go to a solitary area where you won't be disturbed and try to relax for a few moments. I suggest just sitting in a comfortable chair and letting your thoughts effortlessly come and go. Close your eyes if you like and take a few deep breaths to relax. Having a lighted candle and burning some incense may help the mood. Whatever gets you into a relaxed and meditative state is an asset. You should position the crystal in front of you, not too far or too close, but where you can look comfortably into it. Placing it on a small table in front of your chair may be a good idea. You can experiment with the best distances. I prefer to look down at the crystal at an acute angle instead of having it level with my eyes. You can also hold it in your hands, which are placed on your lap. This is what I prefer.

Make sure the candle is some distance from the crystal, because you do not want its reflection in the crystal to be a distraction. Some people put the candle behind where they are sitting. I usually put it in on the side, but far enough away so it does not reflect into the crystal.

I would suggest you have either a white or black plain cloth under the crystal ball so patterns from your clothes or other nearby objects do not reflect into the ball. Keep the room dimly lit. Again, you need to experiment to find the best illumination. If you are sitting and holding the crystal in your hand, make sure you are not straining, because you need to be relaxed to achieve the best results.

It's important not to practice scrying for more than about five or ten minutes at each session, because you don't want to fatigue your retinal nerve or become drained in energy. Try it for about five or ten minutes once or twice a day at most. Don't focus or stare directly at the crystal. Instead, rest your gaze beyond the crystal, as if you are focusing on an object in the distance. This is difficult to explain but easy to do once you try it. It should be done effortlessly and without any strain or effort. That is the key to all of this. Relax and be positive so that you can succeed.

After a few minutes you should start noticing that the area you are looking at in the crystal is getting cloudy. This is a common occurrence and a positive sign that may precede a vision. Subsequent to this, the clouds in the crystal may start to clear or dissipate and you may see visions in the crystal. This is what happened when Dr. John Dee—the famous advisor to Queen Elizabeth I and Enochian Magician—and his scryer, Edward Kelley, when they looked through the crystal ball.[1] If you have no results after about five minutes, just stop and try it again later or the following day. There is no rush, and eventually, with perseverance and patience, you may succeed.

There have been many descriptions from clairvoyants about what happens before they have visions. Some describe the initial and preliminary visual experience as follows:

1. As mentioned, their crystal becomes foggy, cloudy, or milky and after it clears up the person starts seeing visions.
2. The crystal starts to disappear completely and then reappears clearly, at which time the visions begin.

3. Different colors or flashes of light appear in the crystal and then the vision begins.

This is not a comprehensive list of pre-vision phenomena but some of the more common experiences. Your experience may be completely different—there are no right or wrong pre-visual phenomena, which, I believe, are caused by the brain and thus are psychological and not spiritual. These preliminary visions open the door to the real clairvoyant state.

PSYCHIC ENERGY AS IT RELATES TO CLAIRVOYANCE

This may be a good place to comment about the psychic energy involved in scrying and/or any type of clairvoyant or psychic process. I have been involved in research with both Russian and Ukrainian scientists for many years. A top Ukrainian scientist who has been doing psychic research and pyramid research for decades believes, as mentioned earlier, that the energy involved in pyramids, and the energy that mediates psychic phenomena, are one and the same.[2]

This suggests that we may have a psychic or paranormal unified field theory in which one type of energy mediates and is responsible for all psychic, paranormal, and unknown phenomena (like pyramid energy) and once we discover and quantify this we will have many answers for a wide variety of unknown phenomena. I like this because it is consistent with our universal laws. Einstein and others have searched for a unified field theory for physical forces (gravity, electromagnetism, and strong and weak nuclear forces), but no one has successfully derived one equation that describes them all. I hope more physicists and mathematicians in the United States become interested in this area of psychic research. If so, we may discover a "unified psychic phenomena field theory" that will describe how all psychic phenomena works, including clairvoyance, remote viewing, pyramid energy, and ley lines, for instance.

In medieval times many people believed that crystals worked by spirits or angels mediating the psychic information between them and us. That is, crystals draw spirits near us and in some instances into the crystals, and the spirits communicate with us through psychic visions. Please keep in mind that the manner in which the psychic visions appear is different for different people. Also it may be different for the same individual at different times of the day, week, or year. This is because visions are variable and dynamic and each individual experience is unique.

Some have argued that these visions are subjective and it's just the person's imagination or subconscious that is at play. I remember hearing about some interesting research done in the early twentieth century, which demonstrated that two gifted scryers looking into the same crystal saw exactly the same scenes, which demonstrates a clinically reliable standard. Unfortunately there are not many documented cases like this, which seem to point to the fact that scrying may have a reality of its own.

You should be aware of some of the signs of overdoing it when you are practicing scrying so you know when to stop and give it a rest. Some of these signs of overexertion include retinal fatigue, eyes that tear up, a feeling of tightness around the forehead and/or temples, and/or tension in other parts of the body. Anything that causes discomfort should be viewed as a sign to stop and rest.

When you begin the practice of scrying, vary the time of day. In this way you will see if you get better results at a certain time of the day versus another. I recommended scrying in the morning or evening to start with, but experiment with other times to find the optimal time for you.

10
Meditating with Crystals

FACTORS IN CRYSTAL MEDITATION

Often I am asked how best to select and care for crystals. I am also asked about how to meditate with them. Given this, I decided to ask my very good friend and gifted psychic-medium Helene Olsen, whose work I discussed in chapter 7, to contribute to this chapter by offering up her insights, gleaned from many years of working with crystals. Much of this information, especially the meditation technique, was received by her psychically from angels or beings that she communicates with. Helene Olsen also teaches meditation techniques on national radio, television, and the Internet. Here she gives us some basic theory for meditating with crystals.

Each one of us has an energy field that's all around us and traveling through us. It's powered by our chakras (seven major energy centers) and extends all around the outside of our physical bodies and reflects in our aura. We have all had the experience of standing physically next to another person and feeling their energy, or, as we like to say, their "vibes." Sometimes we intuitively feel if another person is feeling happy, sad, calm, angry, or sick, for instance. We are often attracted to people intuitively because we know they are

132

nice or need help. When we create a thought, feeling, idea, or emotion we are creating energy. That is why we "feel" one another. That is also why it is very important to focus on thoughts and ideas that serve your highest benefit. This is the basis of all positive thinking and visualization exercises.

TIPS FOR BUYING CRYSTALS

We will now address recommendations and guidelines for purchasing your own crystal. To me, this is very important because you need to have a crystal that you feel comfortable with—one that you can connect and bond with. There are many places to purchase a crystal. A metaphysical bookshop would be a good place to start. The people who work there may well be kindred spirits, and because of that they may have some good recommendations for you. Museums and science museum stores should also have a good variety, even though their sales people may not be as like-minded as those in the metaphysical bookstore (although you never know!).

You can also buy crystals on the Internet, but I would stay away from this option as you cannot hold them and get a direct psychic impression. Some people can get impressions and psychic feelings by just looking at a photo of a crystal, but this is a rare gift. If you do decide to buy one on the Internet, make sure you can return it if you don't like it or don't feel an energy from it.

Decide beforehand how much money you want to spend, and don't rush the process of selecting the right crystal. I would suggest that you should not spend an exorbitant amount initially. The monetary value of the crystal does not matter, but your psychic relationship to it does. I would suggest a range of approximately ten to fifty dollars. If this is your first crystal, you will most likely be purchasing additional ones in the future so this does not have to be your perfect or dream crystal. Helene makes the following recommendations.

Please make finding your new crystals an up-close-and-personal experience! I think that meeting them in person and kindly introducing yourself is the gentlest way to make a new acquaintance. Find a day when you are relaxed and can concentrate on the task at hand, a day when you have a bit of freedom and are doing fun things. Intend to feel the crystals that you will soon meet. Calmly open your mind and focus on the energy of love radiating from your body to the crystals at hand. As you gently handle them, you will start to feel drawn to one more than another. Some may feel warmer or cooler to you, but only you will know which one is the right one for you. Take some extra time. Use your gentle heart to pay attention and you will be surprised at how this process makes you feel.

The next area we will address is the specific type of crystal to buy—clear, rose, smoky quartz, round, hexagonal, or large or small, for instance. Many books have been written about different crystals for different applications; you can refer to some of these if you like. I personally don't believe that this matters too much initially. Once you become more familiar with scrying, and the different types of crystals available to you, you can then specialize and use certain types of crystals for specific applications. The following are recommendations from Helene.

There is much literature about variants of crystals and their applications. Rose quartz, for instance, is considered to be the premier crystal to use for healing. Go with that, if it resonates with you. You can find lists in many volumes, but I personally don't subscribe to any of them. I believe that each variant of quartz is equally useful, and my personal preference is for clear, natural quartz. Of course, this may be a bit pricier, so keep in mind that all the spots and breaks and colorations of quartz are what add to its magnificent character.

How big should your crystal be? Many people I know choose crystals that are fairly small and fit easily into the palm of their hand. As you work with them and get comfortable you might find yourself choosing larger crystals that may be more the size of your hand. If they are over a certain size, they become somewhat impractical and/or overpowering to work with in daily meditation. If you're working to heal another person and are interested in placing crystals on his or her body as part of the healing procedure, please refer to books on this specific subject. Energy channeled through crystal is magnified and there are many excellent methods of placing crystals on the body that you should investigate.

The first crystal that I purchased for meditation and psychic use was a small crystal ball about two inches in diameter. It fit perfectly into the palm of my hand and felt very warm and comfortable. It was not perfect and had many inclusions, and, in fact, I got a good price on it because it was not a perfect crystal. Others may prefer an elongated or hexagonal crystal, like a wand, or an unpolished crystal that looks like a large rock.

CLEANING YOUR CRYSTAL

Now that you have purchased your crystal, what's the next step? Most crystal experts agree that the crystal should be spiritually cleaned. What that means is that when you obtain a crystal you have no idea of its history and how it has been used spiritually. The vibrations of the previous owner, as well as those persons who frequented the store where you bought it, are on your crystal. You don't want these vibrations on your personal crystal as they may interfere and affect your work with it. So, the next step is to cleanse your crystal, using one, if not more, of the several methods available for so doing. I usually employ two or three of them to be safe. Here are some ways to cleanse your crystal.

1. The simplest and easiest way is to hold the crystal in your hand and dedicate it to the spiritual work that you are going to do with it. Also command that all negative and impure vibrations depart the crystal and that only the good, holy, and God-like energy remain.

I like to light a candle during this ritual as, in my opinion, this empowers the entire ritual. I also suggest that you douse the crystal in incense (I recommend sage incense) as part of the ritual. I use sage as it is a universally known spiritual cleanser, not only of crystals, but of all objects. In a Catholic church, the priest incenses the altar before benedictions to spiritually cleanse the area.

You can buy sage at many New Age bookstores or order it on the Internet. The sage, the candle, and your words of blessing are very effective and are all you need to employ, in most cases. You can also say your own personal prayers over the crystal during this ritual—it personalizes your use of this object.

2. I suggest that if you do the first method and for some reason you feel that the crystal is not purified or all negative vibrations were not removed, then you can follow these instructions to cleanse it. Many years ago someone recommended that I place my crystals in a bag filled with sea salt for several days or even weeks; this is the more traditional way to purify crystals. (Other people soak their crystals for only a few minutes; this is a matter of personal opinion.) You can obtain sea salt at most supermarkets. If you have just purchased your first crystal, you will want to use it right away and not leave it in a bag for days or weeks.

3. An old way to purify a crystal or any ritual object is to bury it in the ground for several days or weeks. Mother Earth is a ground and tends to neutralize negative vibrations, but again you may not want to be without your new crystal for that long of a time. Also, if it is winter, the ground may be frozen and have snow on it.

4. The next method that I will address is, in my opinion, the best. You need to read the following chapter for the exact method and procedure to use, but this is an ancient magical ritual. It takes only a few minutes to do and is known as the Lesser Banishing Ritual of the Pentagram (LBRP). This is discussed in chapter 11. If you add the sage purification ritual, I don't think you could do any better in removing any and all negative and unwanted vibrations.

There are many other methods you can research, but I believe the ones mentioned above are the best and the most efficient. In addition, they are simple and very inexpensive to perform; the only things they require are sage and sea salt.

CARING FOR YOUR CRYSTAL

Now that you own a crystal and it is cleansed from any negative vibrations, Helene also makes some recommendations and suggestions for caring for your crystal.

> Many people enjoy looking at their crystals and feeling their vibrations throughout the day in an open space. Crystals enjoy being "out" in the air and light, but please do not keep them in a place of very direct sunlight for extended periods of time. You may "cleanse" them and purify their vibration by laying them out in direct sunlight for a few hours at a time. Please keep in mind, though, that crystals can act as a magnifying glass, and especially in the case of crystal balls, please make sure that their placement will not start any kind of smoldering! Some people like to lay them out in the peaceful light of the full moon overnight, which has the same purifying effect on the crystal. What I do occasionally is soak the crystals for a few hours in tepid water and a couple of pinches sea salt. This method works just as well as any other. Those who use crystals in various healing modalities often find that this method is the best way to neutralize the energy released and/or transferred by their last client.

PREPARING FOR CRYSTAL MEDITATION

Now that your crystal is cleansed and ready to go you can begin your meditation. Many books have been written about meditating with crystals, and you can also find a plethora of material on this subject on the Internet. You need to find a technique that you are comfortable with and, most importantly, one that will give you the results you are seeking, because that's what this is all about.

The purpose of crystal meditation is to open a connection to the angels and the spiritual world; crystal is the tool for doing so. As mentioned in a previous chapter and because I believe it's worth repeating here, the crystal is not to be idolized—it is just a pointer or a catalyst. The reason we chose quartz crystal is that it seems to be one of the most successful tools in that more people have better results with crystals than with other types of stones or other materials.

Helene offers several methods or procedures for meditating with your crystal. The following text is in her own words. She states how she received information about meditating with crystals, and how you can do the same.

MEDITATING WITH CRYSTALS

Helene Olsen

These crystal meditation techniques were channeled to me, over time, by Pleiadian Light Masters. Pleiadians are divine beings of healing light, traveling on source energy from the fifth dimension. They are presently communicating with many healers, psychics, and intuitives, because they want to assist us in raising our vibrational frequency and elevating mass consciousness. To connect with them, set your intention to communicate and say their name before you begin your crystal meditation. They will welcome your energy!

Meditation is the act of clearing your mind of ego and thought and creating an open or "blank" state of being. Even in its most basic practice, meditation expands your awareness, expanding the energetic field around you and bringing a certain sense of peace to your mind. Thoughts become less overwhelming, and triviality is easier to handle.

Many people have told me over the years that they were not capable of meditating. I've simply found this to be untrue—anyone can learn to meditate. When you are just starting out I believe it's best to learn in a group with other beginners. The reason a group works well is because energy connects. If everyone in your circle or group is focused on being in a relaxed state and letting go of "mind," this energy will be palpable to you and you will more easily be able to use it.

Beginners groups are often offered for free or little cost at healing centers, adult education centers, and hospitals (as part of a community stress reduction class). Your initial goal should be to learn to open that space of no-thought and remain there for fifteen to twenty minutes. More advanced techniques of greater depth are learned from those who have mastered this art if you choose to pursue a deeper level and/or other modalities of meditation.

In meditation, as in all other things in life, *energy follows thought*. This is a very important concept to grasp. Every word you speak, think, and write carries its own energy of creation and manifestation. It's your own intention that creates your mindful reality. In meditation it's important to use the technique of your intention and visualizing your "reality" to bring the positive energy and healing that your mind and physical body call out for. With that said, the following meditation techniques outline the goal for your visualization and thought process in the meditative state.

Crystals carry a very high vibrational frequency. When you have them physically near or on your body they can assist you by being a "battery," or energetic assistant, that helps you to meditate more easily and at a deeper level.

Two-Crystal Meditation

A simple method by which to meditate is to simply choose two small crystals and rest one on each of your upturned palms. Your palms have a sensitive energy area, or chakra, and placing crystals here will help your energy to balance, align, and connect to a higher consciousness while you meditate.

Three-Crystal Meditation

A second method of connecting to crystal vibration is to choose three smaller crystals. Rest one in the palm of each hand and hang the other directly over your third eye, which is the area located in the center of your forehead. You can hang your crystal by wrapping it in wire and leaving a space near the top of the wire to push a cord or string through. Make the cord just slightly smaller than the widest part of your head. In this way you will be able to wear it on top of your head comfortably, with the crystal dangling over your forehead.

Here is how to use the power of your own thoughts to create a connection with your three crystals.

1. Visualize and mentally focus your thoughts on connecting with these three crystals.
2. When you feel comfortable and connected to them, create in your own mind a straight laser beam of white or pink light flowing from each crystal that you hold, connecting that light beam directly to the crystal hanging over your third eye.
3. When this is accomplished, imagine and create the visual of an even wider and stronger beam of light that heads straight up from the crystal on your third eye. At this point, set an intention of connecting to your own true self in higher consciousness.

Merkaba Meditation

In this meditation you will visualize a Merkaba, a shape that is an important figure in sacred geometry. *Merkaba* comes from the Hebrew word meaning "chariot" and "to ride." It was taken by the Hebrews to mean the "Throne Chariot of God" described by the prophet Ezekiel in the first chapter of the Old Testament book of Ezekiel. It is the vehicle with four wheels whose movement is controlled by four living creatures. Each creature has four faces: one side a man, another a lion, the third side an ox, and the fourth side an eagle, and each creature has four wings. Ezekiel's vision is pictured in the drawing in figure 10.1.

In modern times many have symbolized and simplified this vision for meditation by drawing two pyramids intersecting each other. There are many different geometric versions of this but this is one of the most

Fig. 10.1. This image of the Merkaba is taken from a Bible published in 1599.

popular and simplest to visualize for meditation. Some believe that visualizing this symbol in meditation allows them to travel into the heavenly or interdimensional realms.

Fig. 10.2. A contemporary, simplified representation of the Merkaba

As you are preparing to meditate in a chair or on the floor, place four, five, or six crystals in a symmetrical, large circle on the floor. You will be centered physically in this circle. If you are using four crystals, the placement would be one in front of you, one behind you, and one on each side of you.

1. Comfortably seat yourself in the center of this circle.
2. Imagine a brilliant white and/or golden light floating far above your head.
3. Visualize a Merkaba of radiant white light spinning over your crown chakra.

4. Bring that powerful beam of golden white light from far above your head, right through the spinning Merkaba and into your crown chakra.

5. Slowly bring that beam right through the core of your body and visualize it passing through each major chakra.

6. As this divine light comes through your feet, imagine it connecting with each of the crystals around you.

7. Each crystal receives the light and beams its energy right back to the spinning Merkaba above your crown.

In this way, you have effectively created a grid, or cage of energy, around your physical body. While this is happening, divine light continues to pour from above, into the core of your body. You have created a continuous circle! When it's time to leave this meditation, consciously choose to dim the light that's beaming down from above.

In ending a meditation session it is essential to ground your energy. Choose to visualize pulling your energy in through your crown. Then, slowly pull the energy all the way through the core of your body, stopping at your toes. Choose to become aware and awake and slowly open your eyes. You should further ground by clapping your hands or stomping your feet on the floor. When you stand up, do so slowly; you may feel light-headed when exiting a meditative state.

Helene and I hope your meditation using your crystal will be successful and spiritually rewarding. But remember, opening and awakening your spiritual sense, which has been dormant for a long time, takes time and practice. So don't be discouraged but continue with perseverance and no doubt, with time, you will be rewarded.

11
Magical Rituals with Crystals

To carry out the magical meditation in this chapter you should first read the chapters on scrying and meditation. This chapter, which is divided into two practical sections, details a magical meditation I will be teaching you and builds on material found in earlier chapters.

The first section will teach you a technique for creating a magical circle in which all negative energies and vibrations will be blocked out. This technique is called the Lesser Banishing Ritual of the Pentagram. It will provide a very peaceful, relaxing, and quiet context in which you will be able to successfully conduct your meditation. In fact, if all you do is read this first section and use it with the chapter on meditating with crystals, I believe it will enhance and increase your efforts at scrying and meditating with crystals. In addition, and as mentioned in the previous chapter, this ritual can be used to cleanse and purify your crystals.

The second section of this chapter outlines how to alter your state of consciousness in order to enter into a higher spiritual realm, which you will inhabit when scrying and meditating with your crystal.

In undertaking the Enochian Meditation you are calling upon the

144

angels and inviting them to contact you. This magical technique is the only technique that ever worked for me in opening to a higher spiritual consciousness and the higher spiritual realms, because, as stated earlier, I hadn't had much luck initially with scrying and meditating with crystals. However, having said that, I must also state that the Enochian Meditation may not be for everyone, so please use your judgment and follow your instincts here. To enter into a higher realm or spiritual dimension, I always tell people that they should be of stable mind and not have any outstanding psychological problems. If they do, these problems should initially be resolved with the help of a licensed medical professional. I must also state that the author and the publishers of this book are not responsible for the results of this magical ritual and meditation. I believe it's a safe practice, and I personally have conducted it hundreds of times with positive results every time. I would not include it here if I believed it to be dangerous, but we are also charting new ground and do not have all the answers. I have explored many other published techniques for meditating with crystals and do not find that they alter the state of consciousness and body physiology in the significant way that this technique does.

For those of you who want to go deeper into this magical meditation, please refer to my other books, *The Lost Art of Enochian Magic* and/or *Decoding the Enochian Secrets,* wherein I detail the meditation technique in its entirety.

You may be interested in knowing how I decided to incorporate the use of crystal skulls in this magical meditation. I was talking with my good friend Lon Milo DuQuette, who is the world's foremost ceremonial magician and who wrote the foreword to my book *The Lost Art of Enochian Magic.* We were discussing the results of my Enochian Meditation, and Lon knew of my work with crystal skulls. He suggested that I try to use a crystal skull with the Enochian ritual.

I had already considered incorporating a crystal ball into the ritual because one is often used by magicians, but I hadn't considered using my ancient crystal skull. When I tried the meditation using my ancient crystal skull it deepened my altered state by almost a factor of two the first time. It was a profound experience. I then tried using a crystal ball, which also was more effective with it than without it. Thus, I decided to simplify the technique in this book and suggest that crystals or crystal skulls be used with the Enochian Meditation.

Here is some theory on what you will be doing. There are thirty Aethyrs, or heavenly realms, that one can enter using the Enochian Meditation technique; I will be giving you the procedure and directions to enter only the first realm, the Thirtieth Aethyr. If you want to explore the higher realms, I recommend that you get my book *The Lost Art of Enochian Magic*. It contains information that will help you more fully explore the Aethyrs, or spiritual realms, and also comes with a CD to help you with the pronunciation of the terms or Calls used in the meditation.

In Enochian Meditation we can explore the thirty Aethyrs one by one. The Thirtieth Aethyr, which we will be exploring and entering, is the lowest or closest to the Earth and farthest from God; the First Aethyr is the most spiritually elevated one—the one that's closest to God. How many levels a person enters and how deep into them a person can go depends on that individual's level of spiritual development and awareness. The Thirtieth Aethyr, in my opinion, is safe, and most people have no problem entering it successfully.

I believe that the Enochian Meditation technique works by accessing dormant areas in the brain that give us the perception of these heavenly or spiritual realms. I believe people have always had these abilities but they have been lost and need to be reawakened, which is what the Enochian Meditation does. In my opinion, it is one of the best techniques for opening and connecting with the space-time crystal matrix in all its dimensions.

At the end of your magical meditation you will conduct the

Lesser Banishing Ritual of the Pentagram again to close the magical meditation.

THE LESSER BANISHING RITUAL OF THE PENTAGRAM (LBRP)

As stated earlier, the Lesser Banishing Ritual of the Pentagram (LBRP) is a way to purify your environment and protect yourself from any negative energies or entities. The LBRP takes only a few minutes to do. It is so ancient that no one really knows where it originated; it has lasted through eons of time because it's so effective. Almost every time I conduct it, I feel extreme peace and quiet. The atmosphere around me seems pure and I don't have the usual chatter of constant thoughts rattling through my head. I would suggest that even if you don't want to do the actual Enochian Meditation in part 2 of this book, at least try the Lesser Banishing Ritual of the Pentagram and then meditate with your crystal or crystal skull in the protected space you have created for yourself.

🕮 Part One—Preparation and Preliminaries

Before you begin, seat yourself comfortably in a chair near a lighted candle in a dimly lit room. Relax for a few minutes in the chair, and when you are ready, stand up to begin. (The LBRP is done standing up, and the words are said out loud.) It is composed of two parts. First you will do something called the Kabbalistic Cross and then construct the Pentagram of White Light. (The Kabbalistic Cross is similar to the sign of the cross, but the words and directions are different.)

The Kabbalistic Cross
- Stand facing east.
- Visualize the Light of God coming to you and hovering over your

head in a dazzling radiant ball of light.

- Reach up with your right index finger and, touching this ball of light, bring it to your forehead and touch your forehead.
- Say or chant: AH-TEH (Unto Thee . . .).
- Move straight down and touch your chest or stomach and say or chant: MAL-KUTH (. . . the Kingdom . . .). (As you move your finger to each part of your body, visualize the white Light of God moving with you, and at the end you will have a large cross over your body from the white light.)
- Touch your right shoulder and say or chant: VEE-GE-BUR-AH (. . . and the Power . . .).
- Touch your left shoulder and say or chant: VEE-GE DU-LAH (. . . and the Glory . . .).
- Finally, bring your hands together in front of you like in prayer and say or chant: LE-OL-LAM (. . . Forever . . .). AH-MEN.

(I would suggest chanting as it gives this ritual more life and energy. Also, do not repeat the English translations of the words given above in parentheses. This is just for your information.)

The Pentagram of White Light

- Facing east, trace a pentagram in the air. The size doesn't matter, but I usually make it on the large side. I can visualize it as a white, vibrant, dazzling light, or a blue flame (whichever you can see more easily).

Fig. 11.1. Start at the lower left corner and trace the pentagram in the direction indicated until you come back to the starting point.

As illustrated in figure 11.1 below, start at the lower left side of the pentagram and move in the directions indicated in the figure.

- When the pentagram is complete, thrust your right index finger (which you're using as your magic wand) in the center of the pentagram and say or chant: YOD-A-HAY, VAV-A-HAY.
- Turn and face south.
- Make the same pentagram again in the air (starting at the lower left side) and, when completed, thrust your right index finger in the center and say or chant: AH-DO-NAI.
- Turn to the west (notice you're going around a circle in a clockwise direction), trace the pentagram, and when completed, thrust your right index finger in the center and say or chant: E-HI-YAY.
- Turn to the north, trace the pentagram, and when completed, thrust your right index finger in the center and say: AH-GA-LA.
- Turn to the east, and don't trace a pentagram but just thrust your finger in the center of the pentagram you traced initially, thus completing a closed circle of four pentagrams, each one facing a cardinal direction (east, south, west, and north). Visualize this circle and the pentagrams as a vibrant light surrounding and protecting you. These four incantations are names of God.
- Still facing east, stretch out your arms in the form of a cross and chant the following:

    Before me: RA-FAY-EL.

    Behind me: GA-BRE-EL.

    On my right: ME-CHI-ALE.

    On my left: UR-REE-ALE.

    (You're summoning the four archangels of God—Raphael, Gabriel, Michael, and Uriel—for protection.)
- Keep your arms outstretched and continue by saying:

    Before me flames the pentagram.

    Behind me shines the six-rayed star.
- Repeat the Kabbalistic Cross once more, and you're now done with the LBRP.

After you have completed the LBRP, remain standing and pause for a few minutes to soak in the peace and serenity that you, hopefully, are feeling. After this, sit down in your chair and either undertake to scry or meditate with your crystal or continue on to part 2, the Enochian Meditation.

🌿 Part Two—The Enochian Meditation

Remaining seated, read the entire Enochian Call below out loud. It will act like a mantra and produce a resonance in your body and spirit. You can chant it if that makes you feel more in tune with it. The words are broken into syllables, and pronunciation marks are added to indicate long and short vowels.

(Note: The straight line above the vowel indicates a long vowel: ā ē ī ō ū; the caret symbol above the vowel indicates a short vowel: â ê î ô û.)

The Enochian Call of the Thirtieth Aethyr

Mā -drî -iax   Ds praf   (Name of Aethyr, i.e., TEX)   ch(k)īs

Mi-cā-olz Sa-ā-nir Ca- ōs-go, od f ī-sis Bal-zi-zras Ia(ya)-ī-da,

Non-ca(sa) Go-hū-lim, ic(Mīk)-ma A-do-ī-an Mad, I-ā-od

Bli-ōrb, Sâ-ba-o-o-ā-ô-na ch(k)īs Lu-cīf-ti-as pe-rīp-sol, ds

Ab-ra-ās-sa Non-cf(sf) Ne-tā-â-ib Ca-os-gi od Ti-lb Ad-phaht

Dām-ploz, To-ō-at Non-cf(sf) Gmi-cāl-zô-ma L-rāsd Tōf-glo

Marb yār-ry I-doi-go od Tor-zulp ia(ya)-ō-daf Go-hōl,

Ca-ōs-ga Ta-ba-ord Sa-ā-nir od Chris-tê-os Yr-pō-il Ti-ō-bl,

Bus-dir ti-lb No-aln pa-id ors-ba od Dod-rm(rum)-ni Zyl-na.

El-zāp-tilb Parm-gi pe-rīp-sax, od ta Q(K)urlst Bo-o-a-pi-S.

Lnib(Lmb)-m o-v-cho Symp, od Chris-tê-os Ag-tol-torn Mirc

Q Ti-ōb-l Lel. Ton pa-ombd Dil-zmo As-pī-an, od

Chris-tê-os Ag L tōr-torn pa-rāch A-symp, Cord-ziz

Dod-pal od Fi-falz Ls-mnad, od Farg-t Bams O-ma-ō-as.

Co-nīs-bra od A-uâ-vox To-nug, Ors-cāt-bl No-âs-mi
Tab-gēs Levith-mong, un-chi(ki) Omp-tilb Ors. Bagel.
Mo-ō-ô-ah ol cōrd-ziz. L ca-pī-mâ-o Ix-o-māx-ip od
ca-cō-casb Go-sâ-a. Ba-glen pi-i Ti-ān-ta A-bā-bâ-lond, od
fa-ōrgt Te-lōc-vo-vim. Mā-drî-iax Tor-zu O-ād-riax Or-ō-cha(ka)
A-bō-â-pri. Ta-bā-ôr-i pri-āx ar-ta-bas. A-dr(dir)-pan Cor-sta
Do-bix. Yol-cam priā-zi Ar-co-a-zior. Od quasb Q-ting. Ri-pīr
pa-a-oxt Sa-gā-cor(kor). vm-L od prd(pur)-zar ca-crg(cōrg)
Aoi-vē-â-e cor-mpt. Tor-Zu, Za-Car, od Zam-Ran aspt Sib-si
But-mô-na ds Sur-zas Tia Bal-tan. Odo Cicle Q-ā-a, od
oz-az-ma pla-pli lad-nâ-mad.

When you have finished reading the Enochian Call, repeat the names of
the angels or governors of this Aethyr, which are:

Do-zī-nal
Ad-vorpt
Gem-nimb
Ta-ō-â-gla

I suggest you say their names silently. You can move from one angel to
the next when you feel it's right to do so. I usually dwell on the name of
one governor for a few minutes or longer and then go to the next one
for a few minutes. Also know that you don't have to use the governors'
names as a continuous mantra. I like the analogy of going into a room
and calling out the name of a friend. You keep calling out the name until
the friend comes to you, and then you stop. When I feel the presence
of a governor, I usually stop repeating his name. However, if you want to
keep repeating it, that's fine, too. I've done it both ways and find either
way to be effective. This is your personal meditation, and you need to
experiment to see what's right for you.

Once you have established yourself in this Aethyr and made contact
with one or more of the governors in this realm, pick up your crystal and
hold it gently. You can now try scrying with it, following the suggestions

I make in the chapter on scrying. This is the heart of the magical meditation. You are in a deep state and are holding your crystal to amplify and intensify the experience. You also may connect much better with your crystal in this state than in a state of normal waking consciousness. In addition, you have the presence of the angels of this heavenly realm to help you and communicate with you through your crystal.

Experiment and try different things. Initially, I would not do this part of the meditation for more than fifteen or twenty minutes. (You can, however, do it longer as you gain more practice in the technique).

⚜ Part Three—Ending the Meditation

When you're done and want to end the meditation, take a few minutes to relax and come out of your deep rest. This is important, because your body has been in a deep physiological state for fifteen to twenty minutes, and you need at least two or three minutes to readjust. Just stop thinking of the governors' names, and you will gradually come back to your normal state. You can also thank the spirits mentally for their help. You would do this for any friend who showed you around their town after a visit. Use your own words of thanks—whatever feels right to you. On behalf of the angels, I also recite a simple message, giving them license to depart.

License to Depart
(Read silently, or out loud)
O spirits (name the governors here, for instance: Dozinal, Advorpt, Gemnimb, and/or Taoagla), because you have been very ready and willing to come at my call, I hereby license you to depart to your proper place. Go now in peace and be ready to come at my call when requested. May the peace of God be ever continued between you and me.

Do the Closing Lesser Banishing Ritual of the Pentagram

(Stand up and say it out loud)

Sit down and rest for a few minutes before you get up and resume your activities.

Again, I would suggest that you obtain *The Lost Art of Enochian Magic* as there is a CD in the book with the pronunciations of the Lesser Banishing Ritual of the Pentagram and the Enochian Call. It also gives the information for exploring all Thirty Aethyrs.

PART FOUR

*

Atlantis, Aliens,
and
Higher Dimensions

12
Crystals in Atlantis

One of the most important reasons I enjoy writing books is that I learn so much in the process. Most authors begin with an idea and then generate a proposal that they send to the publisher to consider. Usually, the final book is different from what was envisioned in the original proposal because as the research progresses, new knowledge and ideas are obtained that may change the original preconceived ideas of the author.

This happened to me in a significant way during the writing and research of this book. As the research unfolded and determined what its contents would be, I continued to apply scientific rigor to my subject. I always try to separate truth from fiction in my work. Many speculative claims have no basis in fact at all but are perpetuated because they are accepted at face value. Unfortunately, I found this to be true when writing this chapter, the topic of which is the lost continent of Atlantis.

I like to think that I have read most of the important books that have been published on the subject of Atlantis in the past hundred years. It's so fascinating to consider that in Earth's history there may have existed a large, mysterious continent that had advanced technology, perhaps even more advanced than what exists today. In addition, is it possible that the people on this lost continent may have possessed psychic ability and powers that we do not have today? Some people believe the misuse of these powers led to the downfall of the Atlantean civilization and the sinking of the continent.

The search for Atlantis has excited the treasure hunter and the archaeologist, both of whom have tried to locate artifacts from this continent. It has also attracted the study and interest of people of all professions and interests—it is an adventure into the unknown. Historically we first hear of this continent from the writings of Plato in his dialogues *Timaeus* and *Critias,* written in the fourth century BCE. Plato states that its location was in the Atlantic Ocean in front of the Pillars of Hercules (west of Gibraltar) and it flourished around 10,000 BCE. Its name in Greek means Island of Atlas.

It was composed of a confederation of kings and princes and had a strong military and naval power, which made many conquests in the Mediterranean area. The island had thick forests and diverse kinds of animals including elephants, which were not known in the Americas at that time. Atlantis was laid out in three series of concentric circles, land and water alternating with bridges that connected the land areas. Various legends propose either a large temple or pyramid at the center of its central, circular landmass. At its center, the pyramid or temple had a large crystal, which was the power source of Atlantis.

In some legends this crystal or power source is what caused its demise by its accidental or purposeful misuse. Some people postulate that the crystal was some type of transducer and obtained its energy from outer space—the sun or the stars—or possibly from the center of the Earth.

Plato claimed that Atlantis was destroyed by an earthquake and the entire continent sank in one day. We do not know if Plato derived his writings about Atlantis from facts or from myth. It might be the case that he made up the entire story. Plato wrote that Atlantis, located "in front of the Pillars of Hercules," was a great naval power that had conquered many parts of Western Europe and Africa nine thousand years before the time of Solon. This would have been approximately 9600

BCE. After a failed attempt to invade Athens, Atlantis sank into the ocean "in a single day and night of misfortune."

CRYSTAL TECHNOLOGY ON ATLANTIS?

In my research into the continent of Atlantis, as per the story of Plato's Atlantis above, I frequently came across references to crystals. Again, the most common story is that at the center of Atlantis, in the main temple or building, there was a large crystal that was the source of their power and technology. Not only did this unusual crystal produce the energy they needed, but it also could be used as a powerful weapon.[1]

Numerous theories and ideas abound on the origins of this crystal. Some researchers believed it was developed and manufactured by Atlantian scientists. Other researchers believe it came from an alien race from outer space, and still others believe that it was produced psychically; it materialized out of nowhere from psychic energy. Some postulate that it may have been produced by a very ancient culture on Earth, which was technologically advanced. Passed down through time, it eventually found its way to Atlantis.

There are so many unsubstantiated stories about the search for Atlantis that I would like to describe one I heard years ago. A person who was scuba diving found some ruins under water, which he believed were from Atlantis. One structure he observed appeared to be a giant pyramid. He noticed an opening in the pyramid, which he entered. After swimming through this narrow pathway, it eventually opened into a chamber in which there was a crystal skull. The scuba diver supposedly took this skull. Reports have trickled down through the years about this skull, which is rumored to be kept in a safe somewhere. This is a very imaginative story and, if true, it would be my hope that this skull could one day be produced for scientists to study. As far as I know, it never has. There are many such stories and unfortunately, without proof, they remain just stories.

Interest in Atlantis faded somewhat but then was renewed in 1882 when Ignatius Donnelly published the classic book *Atlantis, The Antediluvian World*. The story about how Donnelly wrote this book is interesting. Donnelly was a U.S. congressman from Minnesota and also a state senator. It's believed that after he lost reelection he spent much time in the Library of Congress researching different topics. Atlantis was one of those topics, and he turned this interest into the above-mentioned book. In it he compared similarities among Egyptian and South American cultures, including like-sounding place-names. Atlantis was the source and the link for these similarities.

Many other famous individuals also wrote about Atlantis, including the occultist and founder of theosophy, H. P. Blavatsky, and the famous seer Edgar Cayce.[2] Atlantis appears quite frequently in the past-life readings that Cayce would do for people. Cayce is also known to have predicted that a section of Atlantis would reappear or submerge in the late twentieth century near Bimini in the Bahamas.

Oddly enough, a structure *was* discovered on the floor of the Atlantic Ocean, and it has been dubbed the Bimini Road. Some geologists believe this is a man-made structure and may be the remnants of a road from Atlantis. Most academic geologists do not accept this view, however, but believe the structure was produced by natural forces in the ocean.

Cayce also said that Atlantis had a high level of technology, far surpassing what we have today. He, too, claimed it used a large crystal as its power source, and the misuse of this power led to the destruction of Atlantis. It is also very interesting that Cayce claimed that this crystal used by the Atlanteans for their power source sunk to the bottom of the Atlantic Ocean with the entire continent, but it is still active today. Many persons speculate that it is the explanation for the strange phenomenon that occurs in the Bermuda Triangle, the area where Cayce believes Atlantis sunk. It's frustrating that no real evidence of Atlantis exists, but perhaps some written records about it will be discovered in a hidden chamber of the Great Pyramid or in the Sphinx, as Edgar Cayce predicted.

Other legends regarding the fall of Atlantis claim that certain of its priests had a high level of psychic power that they abused and this is what led to the destruction of Atlantis. Some legends claim this crystal could levitate large objects, and thus large structures could be built in Atlantis with ease. Before Atlantis sank it is believed that some of its most learned scientists and priests were sent to distant lands in ships to preserve their knowledge and culture so it would not be lost. Some scholars believe that Egyptian civilization was based on a culture brought to them by the priests of Atlantis. Was the Great Pyramid built by levitation, and, if so, where did this technical knowledge come from?[3]

An interesting area of research is the discovery of evidence of Atlantis in other parts of the world, such as Central and South America, which it would have bordered. Some scholars point out that there are mustaches on several ancient statues in Central America. Interestingly, the indigenous men of this region of the world did not have mustaches. This anomaly is believed to be evidence of contact with Atlanteans. Scholars also cite extant references to elephants in the Mesoamerican culture prior to the time of Columbus. (There were no elephants in Central America prior to Columbus.) Most archaeologists reject these suggestions and explain these anomalies other ways, but a question lingers in regard to contact between the continent of Atlantis and the Mesoamerican cultures. Legends purport the existence of other continents that have also vanished; these include Mu and Lemuria. Supposedly they existed on the other side of the world, but again the same arguments hold true about whether they really existed or are mere myths that have no basis in reality.

CONCLUSIONS

Unfortunately, after all my reading and research, I had to come to the conclusion that there is currently no solid proof or evidence that the continent of Atlantis ever existed. There is no solid historical, archaeological, or scientific evidence at this time. Many objects are claimed to be Atlantean in origin; however, to the best of my knowledge none of them have been scientifically tested to show their age or prove that Atlantis was their place of origin. Many of them turn out to be artifacts from other known, ancient cultures.

The original location of Atlantis is another critical issue. Its location has been speculated to be at various points all over the globe, or at least in every sea or ocean as far north as the Arctic and as far south as the Antarctic—and every place in between. The plethora of legends from many different cultures attest to potential diversity of locales. In addition, many well-known, gifted psychics, such as Edgar Cayce, claim Atlantis did exist and have been able to see some of its history through clairvoyance. Even though my personal opinion is that Atlantis did at one time exist as a continent, we need to discover some artifacts or structures that are proven to be from this continent before the academic community will take Atlantis seriously.

13
Crystals in
Alien Implants

DO ALIENS EXIST?

Is there any truth to the claims of the existence of UFOs and the abduction of humans by aliens? There have been innumerable UFO sightings throughout history. Some believe certain biblical stories originated from UFOs, such as the experience of Ezekiel in the Old Testament.[1] UFOs have even been seen by thousands of people at the same time and have been picked up on radar. The statistics of the number of Americans who believe in the existence of UFOs is extremely high and growing all the time. Many claimed alien abductions have been shown to be credible by the use of hypnosis and polygraph tests. I personally believe there is enough evidence and validity on this subject so as to be able to explore it in a scientific and objective manner. I have been fortunate to personally know two of the most well-known and credible abductees of all time. I have obtained important information from one of them about their claims concerning alien implants. These claims have never before been published.

ALIEN IMPLANTS

An alien implant is an object or device that is placed in a specific part of the human body by an alien after an abduction incident. In many cases, but not all, the abductee is taken aboard the alien ship, placed on a table for examination, and a small object is inserted into a specific part of the body—usually a hand, foot, leg, arm, or ear, although it may be in almost any area. The size of the claimed implants varies from the size of a pea to as long as an inch in length. They are made of unknown material.

Some of these "implants" have been removed and tested and have turned out to be cartilage or membranous material. Other "implants" have turned out to be metal or some other inert substance. To the extent of my knowledge, none of the "implants" that have been removed and tested have proved to be composed of materials or elements not of this world.

Many UFO researchers question the purpose of these implants. There are many theories, which include that they exist to monitor the individual's physiology, their environment, and/or even as a way to exercise mind control over an individual. The common thought is that they are a kind of transceiver (a device that both transmits and receives information) that the aliens can use to monitor and control some aspect of the human and their environment. Thus, in a sense, it may be some sort of tracking device.

Some abductees also claim that these implants resemble a crystal. In addition to this claim, several abductees have attested that, when they were on board the UFO, they observed that large crystals were a component of the craft. They believe the crystals were the source of the craft's propulsion and navigation, and possibly the source of the craft's energy.[2]

An Abductee's Testimonial

I have decided to focus on the experiences of one abductee and her experiences with alien implants. This person and her mother, who also was abducted, are two of the most well-known UFO abductees of all time, and their experiences have been well documented. The other reason I selected this person is that I have known her for several years and can vouch for her honesty and integrity.

I am referring to Becky Andreasson and her mother, Betty. The abduction of Betty Andreasson (known as the Andreasson Affair) is one of the most well-known, well-documented abductions in UFO history.[3] It happened one winter evening in 1967, at Betty's home in Massachusetts. The mother of seven children, Betty was in the kitchen of the house; the rest of the family was in the living room. Becky is the oldest child; she was eleven at that time.

All of a sudden, through a screened porch on the back of the house, Betty noticed a pulsating light in the window. She looked out and saw five alien creatures approaching. The aliens entered the porch, and as they approached the door she could not believe what happened. They passed right through the door, without opening it, and appeared inside the kitchen. They immediately put her entire family, who were in the living room, in suspended animation and established psychic communication with Betty.

She began to be worried about her family being in this trance state, which the aliens sensed, so in order to show Betty that her family was not in harm's way, they released Becky from suspended animation. Becky remembers all of this to this day. Betty was then taken outside to where a small craft, about twenty feet in diameter, had landed in their backyard. She was taken aboard, after which time the small craft ascended and eventually merged or docked with a much larger craft that was high in the sky. Betty was escorted out of the small craft into the larger one. One of the first things they did to her was to subject her to a physical examination. She remained on this craft for quite some time and was returned home about four hours later. When she got home, she noticed that the family was still in a state of suspended animation. The family was put to bed in this state and then the aliens left.

Over the next ten years Betty continued to be abducted and, as mentioned previously, her entire story is told in a series of five books by the well-known UFO investigator Raymond Fowler.[4] Becky was also subsequently abducted as a child; her story is told in book five of this series. Both Betty and Becky claim that the aliens implanted devices in them, either for the purposes of monitoring them or in order to collect data. Becky believes that these implants are similar to our quartz crystal on Earth but have some kind of living or energetic quality, a life of their own, so to speak.

The first implant that Becky received occurred about ten years ago when she was living in Glouster, Virginia. One morning she woke up to the sound of her dogs barking loudly. They were obviously very disturbed by something. Becky got up and let them out and they ran outside around a corner of the house. Becky lost sight of them, but they were still barking. All of a sudden the barking stopped, almost as if the dogs had been frozen in time.

As Becky stood by the door she looked up to her right and saw a bright light. She became frozen, as if in a state of suspended animation, but she was conscious of what was going on. She felt something under her arm and when she looked down, she saw a strange tubing of a bluish white color that had entered her body under her armpit. She sensed that through this tube something was being introduced into her body. After a few minutes the tubing was removed and she saw another big flash of light. Then out of the corner of her eyes, she saw someone wearing a white gown. In slow motion she turned to see what she describes as a grey alien about four feet tall standing in back of her. All of a sudden, time seemed to start again. The dogs began to bark, and the tubes and the alien were gone. What had just happened seemed like a dream to her.

At this point the dogs ran back into the house and into the

bedroom as fast as they could; both appeared to be scared. Becky followed them and sat at the bottom edge of her bed, looking out the bedroom window. She lit a cigarette and puzzled over what was happening when suddenly she saw a huge vertical beam of lilac-colored light outside her bedroom window. It appeared to be moving upward and then, all of a sudden, it disappeared.

Had the beam originated from the craft as it was taking off? Becky felt unable to move and therefore didn't look out the window to find out. She estimates that the beam may have been about three feet wide and was present only for a matter of seconds. Everything appeared to have happened in slow motion.

Becky then fell asleep. Upon awakening the next morning, she slipped into her regular morning routine, not thinking about what had taken place the night before. But something happened very shortly to bring her back to that reality. When she got into shower, she noticed a small bump in her right armpit, the size of a pea, in the exact same area that the tube had been inserted. At this point the memories of the previous evening came flooding back to her in a very vivid fashion. The bump didn't hurt or bother her until sometime later. Over the next few weeks, strange things started to occur.

The pea-size object started to vibrate at certain times and also to move. It did not do this constantly but only at certain times, and its movements were very slow. It seemed to be moving up through her shoulder and then started moving down through the arm toward her hand. At times when it vibrated she lost function of her arm and dropped things that she was holding. It also sometimes caused a twitch that lasted several minutes. Becky did not actually feel it move but noticed that, over a two-week period, it had slowly moved toward her hand. It finally wound up *in* her hand, ending at the knuckle area between the index and middle finger.

Many other people—family, friends, and strangers—could feel the ball in her hand, so there was obviously something there. She never went to a doctor and truly believes that what the aliens put in her was for her personally. She also knew the doctors would not believe her story. I asked her again recently why she was convinced that the ball was a crystal-like substance, and her reply was that its vibration convinced her that it was a crystal-type of substance.

Becky also told me of a second implant that she believed she had received in her foot many years ago. After her abduction she noticed a mark on the back of one of her heels. It felt like some kind of shard. It wasn't glass. To her, it felt like crystal. This object, like the smaller one, also vibrated at times. She believed it was also transmitting and receiving information, or energy. Then one day she felt this object start to move outward, toward the surface of her heel. She noticed a part of the object starting to protrude from her skin. She tried pulling it out with a tweezers but it just pulled itself back in, like it had a life of its own. Over the next few days it continued to vibrate on and off, and Becky decided to try to pull it out again but couldn't because it wasn't protruding far enough from the skin for her to be able to grasp it with the tweezers.

The implant started to hurt her when she walked, and this began to irritate her to no end because she felt there was nothing she could do about it. Finally, she took her cigarette lighter and torched the object, which was then protruding slightly from her heel. It instantly absorbed the flame, started to burn, then fizzed with blue light and exploded. She said that it just seemed to burn itself up and disappear and then it was completely gone from her body.[5]

It was as if the object just drank the fire in and was consumed internally, which reminds me of spontaneous human combustion. It was miraculous that she didn't get any burn marks from either the lighter or the object burning up. Any and all marks that had been on her feet from the implant were also gone. It was, she said, as if the object had never even been there. One interesting side note of this is that recently her father bought an EMF (electromagnetic field) meter. As discussed previously, these meters are used by ghost hunters to detect the presence of ghosts or spirits in the area they are exploring.

To refresh, EMF meters detect changes in the electromagnetic field, which would happen, for example, if a ghost moved through it. Some meters have needles that are deflected when a change is detected, and the greater the electromagnetic field change, the greater the deflection. This is measurable and quantitative. The simpler EMFs have several lights in a row and each one has a different color. The greater the field strength, the more lights light up.

Becky's father checked the areas of Becky's body where she believed the implants were, and the EMF meter went off over all of these areas at a very high strength. This should not happen. I have an EMF meter, and I've never gotten any deflections by putting it on my body or anyone else's, unless that person had a cell phone or other electronic device on them. Your body does not emit any significant EMF that would register on these meters.

When Becky's father, Bob, was checking one of her implants, the meter indicated a large change in EMF. Then, shockingly, the implant started to move away from the meter. Bob followed it with the meter as it moved more deeply into her body, as if to try to avoid detection by the meter.[6] This is very strange and would lead me to believe that the implants can monitor and react to outside stimuli.

I must mention that Becky also claims that she was abducted as a child. She said that the aliens, at that time, taught her a special, or angelic, language as she calls it. I have copies of this language, which she wrote out for me. It really is unique, and I believe it may be related to humankind's original ancient language, one for which we don't have any records. What's so fascinating is that when Becky was writing down the language, her implant would vibrate so intensely that she had to cease writing.[7] It seemed it had some resonance to this language.

We are left with a very strange and unusual story from a person whom I have known personally for many years, and I honestly believe she is telling the truth. I also believe these things really happened to her and are not a product of her imagination. She didn't wish these things upon herself. Why she was selected by the aliens to be subjected to all of this is a mystery; however, it is a mystery that she and I continue to try and solve together. I'm hopeful that we will eventually recover a sample of one of these alien implants from her, which I could then scientifically test to determine if this material is not from this world.

14
The Space-Time Crystal Matrix

I was trying to come up with a term that would describe my theory about how crystals work in the metaphysical and spiritual sense and the phrase "Space-Time Crystal Matrix" popped into my head. I instantly realized that this term completely explains my theory.

WHAT IS A CRYSTAL MATRIX?

We know what a crystal is. Its main property is that it is symmetrical and has a repetitive crystal lattice pattern, as seen in x-ray diffraction. How a crystal lattice is formed is really a miracle of nature. Atoms and molecules come together and not only do they form specific molecular combinations but also a beautiful three-dimensional structure that is well ordered, repetitive, and symmetrical. Not only is it perfectly ordered from a molecular point of view, but its final product is an incredibly beautiful mineral that stimulates our innermost being or spirit. I believe that a quartz crystal transcends the material plane, into the spiritual realm, and thus is multidimensional as we will discuss.

The concept of a crystal matrix implies a connective structure. What does it connect? I believe it connects the physical and spiritual realms and allows communication between them. It can also have the property of being a communications device of some sort, like a telephone to other realms. The communications can be within our physical realm but also between other worlds and dimensions. I believe this is how prayer works as well. We send our energies to help others, and this energy connects with them on a spiritual plane. Our thoughts and energy move through a matrix, a prayer matrix.

The crystal matrix is special in that it can act as a communications device with the physical realm, the spiritual realm, angels, and maybe even God himself. We don't know exactly what we are dealing with here except that it is something that exists in a higher reality, a higher dimension so to speak. It's my belief that a crystal matrix is composed of both physical and spiritual matter. The physical part is the quartz crystal that we see and touch, but it also has an extension into other dimensions. The Space-Time Crystal Matrix has a unique connection to both the physical and the spiritual worlds; it has special properties and abilities that we can utilize for our benefit and that of others. Rocks and minerals are beautiful and have spiritual natures too, but I don't believe they are extensive communications matrixes as crystals are.

This multidimensional connection is what is so mystical about crystals. When we look at a crystal, we not only see its beauty and/or the physical aspect of it but also something subconscious, which calls us into the presence of a higher consciousness or God. Why do you think psychics since the beginning of time have used quartz crystal for divination and for contacting the spiritual worlds? They did not use shale or granite or limestone, but quartz crystal.

The church, in a sense, has tried to develop spiritual matrixes for ages. Icons, relics, Stations of the Cross, rosaries, candles, statues, and other physical objects have traditionally been used by the church to help one connect with God. For some people these objects and practices can be very helpful in connecting with God. In the Catholic faith as in other religious denominations, the Eucharist is the primary matrix used to connect us to Jesus.

I must tell you that I have been a member of many different religions, both traditional and so-called New Age, since the 1960s. One of the most profound religious experiences I can have is to be present in front of the Blessed Sacrament during its exposition. At certain times of the year and on special holy days, the Catholic Church displays the consecrated host in a ciborium for the faithful to pray in front of. Frequently I would go into a state of near ecstasy in the presence of the host, at which point I would remember what a clairvoyant had once said to me: that she saw an infinite path from the host to God.

All of this is a big mystery, one that I believe the church is not aware of. And yet even if they were aware of it, no doubt they wouldn't acknowledge the metaphysical aspect of the consecrated host, because they don't accept the basic premise that psychic phenomena occurs in their rituals. This is unfortunate, because the rituals of the church are full of metaphysical meaning.

The Space-Time Crystal Matrix imparts a direct connection, like a telephone, to other dimensions if you know how to use it. It's wonderful to have a physical object that can bring us closer to God. Some people may connect better with standard religious icons, some of which I have listed above. Everyone has different spiritual natures and thus different spiritual paths. My favorite Sufi saying is: "There are as many paths to God as souls in the world." Our goal in life is to come back to God, to be present with God, and eventually become one with him. I believe crystals and the Space-Time Crystal Matrix can help us with this goal. How do we connect with this Space-Time Crystal Matrix? In real life we connect with someone by spending time with them, thereby getting to know them. In the same way, we should spend time with our crystals and use them in prayer and meditation.

QUANTUM CRYSTALS

I relayed a story in chapter 5 about a person who believed that the Mitchell-Hedges crystal skull was supposed to be used for evil purposes.

His presence produced poltergeist phenomena in the house in which the skull was located. Frank Dorland, the owner of the house, believed that the energy was derived from the observer or person looking at and/ or touching the skull, which is what happens in the world of quantum physics: the observer affects an outcome.

This doesn't make apparent sense in the normal world we live in. For example, if we drop a ball and measure its acceleration, it will fall at a rate of thirty-two feet per second squared. What this means is that every second it will increase its velocity by thirty-two feet per second. At three seconds its velocity will be ninety-six feet per second. In a simple physics formula this would be demonstrated in an equation ($v = at$) whereby the "v" represents velocity, "a" represents acceleration, and "t" represents time. Thus, if the acceleration is a constant, one can always calculate how *fast* the ball is falling depending on how *long* it has been falling. Generally speaking, the constant doesn't change no matter where you are on Earth, and it doesn't matter who conducts the experiment, or who is watching it. This is true for most laws of physics. Assuming that the experiment is done the same way every time and that it's done correctly, the results will be the same no matter who conducts it.

How does the world of quantum physics fit into this paradigm, especially when we assume that an observer can influence and/or change any given outcome? If we understand that this quantum effect only occurs at the subatomic level, we will also understand why we don't *see* these quantum effects in our everyday world. In other words, we are not capable of perceiving the subatomic essence of our universe. Given all of this, the value of the above-referenced acceleration experiment would then differ, depending on whether someone was watching the experiment. You may not think this is logical, but it *is* the way that quantum physics operates.

Bringing this analogy back to crystals and crystal skulls, I believe that when people of good intentions meditate with an ancient crystal skull, calmness, love, and unity prevail. Conversely, when people who are *not* of good intention interact with crystals and crystal skulls, disharmony and strange phenomena occur. This is how quantum theory, operating on a subatomic level, pertains to crystal use.

String Theory as It Pertains to Crystals

At this level, a discussion of string theory is pertinent. String theory posits that all matter and energy is composed of small, vibrating strings of energy. This would also be subject to quantum laws. Given this, the entire crystal lattice of atomic and subatomic particles are projected into other dimensions so that we have a vibrating composite of super strings that may connect and affect all crystals in the universe, and perhaps all minds as well.

It's interesting that for string theory to work there have to be additional dimensions other than the three spacial and single-time dimensions of our normal world. Physicists, in fact, believe there have to be at least six additional spacial dimensions for string theory to work, thus a total of nine spacial and one time dimension for a total of ten dimensions (some even postulate a total of 26 dimensions). Stephen Hawking and Michio Kaku are two well-known physicists who promote and discuss string theory.

Many mathematicians and physicists do not believe in the tenets of string theory, which is still being studied and researched. I believe string theory is the most logical and reasonable way to explain these phenomena and hope more research is done in this area. But for now, I accept the hypothesis that crystals communicate through other dimensions and even interact with our mind. Before I end this discussion, keep in mind that nine of these ten dimensions are spatial dimensions. What if time dimension is also involved? Then the idea that crystals can give us information from the past and the future could be explained and would have a scientific basis. This really gives us something to think about. Perhaps new advances in science will give us methods to test these hypotheses.

What I have discussed so far is all speculation but I would like to continue to speculate as to how I believe this may work scientifically.

The key to explaining it may have something to do with the theory of general relativity. Einstein showed that space and time are interrelated and by accelerating near the speed of light, we can slow time. Conversely, if we theoretically travel faster than the speed of light, we can go back in time. My idea is that the crystal structure is actually a combination of space and time. We only see the space part of it, but if we could penetrate its secrets, we would know that a time aspect also exists. So, maybe we could travel through time using crystals if we knew how. Maybe the people of Atlantis and other ancient civilizations knew this secret.

CRYSTALS AS RECORDING DEVICES

Some people believe that crystals are capable of recording everything they have been exposed to since their formation—millions of years ago in the earth—until the present. Thus, when someone looks into a crystal he or she may be able to see history if they know how to unlock this secret. (Please see Richard Shafsky's account of this with the Mayan crystal skull, discussed in the appendix.) Perhaps if and when we see alien worlds and strange dimensions in the crystal it's because the crystal is projecting those realms to us. That would render the crystal skull a multidimensional space-time device. Again, were the ancients aware of this, but that knowledge, today, is lost? Can we rediscover this information? I don't think we will discover it merely by using a scientific approach; we need to employ a spiritual and metaphysical approach as well.

Because crystals exist in multidimensions and we can only see the three-dimensional projection of them, in how many other dimensions of space do they exist? We have no idea, but let me give you an example that may help illustrate hyperspace to you. Visualize a two-dimensional world, which only has length and width, no depth, like the surface of a table. On this surface two-dimensional creatures live. That means their movements and what they can observe are limited to the surface of the table. If you place a cube on the surface they can only observe where it contacts the surface; the height is outside their viewing area or perception. Thus they do not know it is a cube but see it as a flat square. Thereby they only perceive two of the three dimensions of this object. However, if a ball is placed on this two-dimensional surface and moves through it, the creature would see the point where the ball initially touches that surface. Then, as the ball moves through that surface, the creature would see a small circle that gets larger and larger and then becomes smaller and smaller until it forms a dot and disappears as it passes through their plane of observation.

The Enochian Magic meditation that I have outlined earlier in the book allows you to enter the higher spiritual realms and access the higher dimensions of the crystal. As an analogy, instead of merely exploring the crystal from a two-dimensional surface—as in our example above—one can go above it and below it to explore it in all of its dimensions.

In this book I have included many facts about quartz crystal and also much speculation about its metaphysical and spiritual purposes. I hope I have made the differences clear. I believe that it's fine to speculate as long as the readers or listeners understand that is exactly what it is. If the speculation is based on some scientific fact or principle, even better. I have tried to base mine on scientific principles whenever possible. I believe speculation is the key to invention and innovation in both science and engineering. Leonardo Da Vinci, Albert Einstein, and others speculated about the physical world and arrived at revolutionary discoveries. But they also tested their unproven theories using the scientific method.

Unfortunately, not all paranormal phenomena can be tested this way, but I think we need to apply it whenever possible. I hope this book stimulates people to imagine, visualize, and hypothesize new ideas and also look for ways to test them. This is how discoveries that change our lives and the world are made. Just think of the communications field, which is comprised of the telegraph, the telephone, recording devices, computers, and lasers, among other things. Someone first imagined what it would be like to send words or sounds to distant locations without physically being there. This started the communications explosion—look where we are today!

Imagination is the key to invention. Einstein used to daydream and that is how he came up with his theory of relativity. He tried to image what it would be like to be riding on a beam of light and what effect this would have. He called his daydreams thought experiments, but they were essentially daydreams. So, please keep on thinking, imagining, creating, and daydreaming about our world and our universe, and maybe someday you will come up with a discovery that will change the world!

My Life
with Quartz Crystals

Many times I find a book on the shelf at my favorite bookstore that I think I'd be interested in reading in order to learn more about a certain topic. I hope that when I finish the book I will be more knowledgeable and confident about the subject about which I've been reading.

I actually hope this is not the case for you when you finish this book. I hope it generates more questions than it answers, stimulates new ideas for you, and challenges what you initially believed. I hope it will make you realize how little we really know about crystals and crystal skulls. I want it to open new thought patterns and new ways of perception for you. I started on this journey with an open mind and didn't know how it would end. I am still on this journey and hope to discover more as time goes on.

What is so much fun about all this is that we cannot say with certainty that we have definitive answers for much of this, and that's why we need new and innovative research and ideas from people like you. We have to stop thinking inside the box and think of unlimited possibilities instead. Of course, the final test is the results of the experiments and data generated, which will either prove or disprove our theories. Too many people go to one extreme or the other. Some people—and unfortunately I see this in many people that we refer to as New Agers—accept almost every theory and idea as long as it sounds cool, exciting, or strange. On the other hand, many academic researchers are so set in their respective belief system that they aren't open to or won't even consider the existence of another realm or world. They limit their view to only the physical world and reject the notion of a psychic or spiritual realm.

I take the middle ground. I am open and even believe in the psychic and spiritual realm, but I also realize I must be critical and scientific in deciding what to believe. I freely address this area and study it but always try to keep a scientific and skeptical attitude. It is okay to speculate as long as you realize that you are speculating. The next step is to always test your hypothesis and see how the data and results tally. It's in this spirit of being open but yet critical that I feel the most progress will be made in the study of the paranormal and psychic realms.

The metaphysical properties of quartz are just one aspect of this study, and I believe we will eventually come up with a psychic or paranormal unified field theory in which one universal law will explain all psychic and paranormal phenomena, just like Einstein looked for a universal field theory or the theory of everything in which one equation explained all physical phenomena.

I first fell in love with quartz crystals when I was a very small boy, and I have continued this love affair to the present time. What did I learn in all this time? Actually, I am more convinced of the incredible properties of quartz, both physically and spiritually. I believe it is important to our spiritual development, both as individuals, and for the planet as a whole. I hope my love affair with quartz has rubbed off on you after reading this book. If that is the case, I feel I have accomplished something. We have only begun to scratch the surface in unraveling the mysterious properties of quartz. Maybe you will discover something that nobody else has.

My concluding advice and suggestion for you is that you keep an open mind, ask questions, and be creative in your thinking, but always try to be critical and analytical and apply the scientific method whenever possible. This will keep you in the middle ground and hopefully you will not be swayed by every new idea or be closed-minded to investigating new and exciting areas of research.

May God Be With You as you continue on your spiritual quest!

Richard Shafsky's Story of the Mayan Crystal Skull

*[**Authors Note:** I personally know Richard Shafsky and believe him to be an honest and credible person. Unfortunately, I cannot confirm or verify his story as I did not witness it firsthand. I leave it to readers to decide for themselves.]*

In 1974 I was the operations manager of a large storage warehouse in California. We were in the midst of a strike, and some enraged union members had obliterated tracking numbers, moved pallets around, and torn identification numbers off crates so that we couldn't locate and retrieve shipments. It was my assignment to find a shipment worth approximately three million dollars in a building the size of a football field, which was chock full of crates and boxes.

I was complaining about the impossibility of this task to a friend who suggested that I ask his dad where to find the shipment; apparently his father was psychic. Having nothing to lose, I called my friend's father, Nick Nocerino, and presented him with my dilemma. When I had finished speaking, Nick did a blessing and then proceeded to "tune in." He told me what he saw: a red flashing light coming to a halt in front of a certain set of numbers, which he relayed to me.

Immediately after the call I got back on my forklift and drove through the warehouse and found the aisle number that Nick had referenced. I turned into that aisle and there was the lost shipment! Later I found out that Nick's psychic abilities had helped U.S. Intelligence locate Nazi prison camps during World War II. That was my introduction to Nick, who I was to be friends with for life.

At our first face-to-face meeting, Nick did a psychic reading for me, during which he couldn't stop grinning. He pulled out a photocopy of the Mayan crystal skull to show me. He then asked me if I had ever seen this object before. I had not. "Well, you will," was his response. He said that I would come in contact with it in Mexico and that he and I would work together to bring it back to the United States. This was a bit of a stretch for me, but nevertheless I would end up, over the next two years, learning from Nick all about crystals, portals, and crystal skulls. At one point he gave me a crystal that he had found under a pyramid in Egypt during World War II when he had left his army encampment to explore the pyramids, for which he was reprimanded severely. Being friends with him and learning from Nick about the paranormal at his knee was a lot of fun and a great avocation for me.

One day I was called to go to Mexico on a new business venture that involved some manufacturing work I was doing. At a business meeting with Mexican and Mayan representatives, I incidentally happened to move the crystal that Nick had given me from my coat pocket to my bag. One of the Mayans at the table, Francesco Reyes, observed this but said nothing. Later that night he appeared at my door. When I let him into the room he made tracks to the crystal, where it was sitting on my bed.

He peered into it and then exclaimed, "Pyramid Egypto!" I looked down at it and in it was an image of the Mayan skull. In the next moment this image had vanished, to be replaced with one of Nick smoking a pipe. Francesco then uttered the word "Mentalista" before bowing and leaving the room. I looked back at the crystal. The image of Nick was now gone. In its stead was one of Nick and Francesco together. I had no idea what any of this meant, but apparently contact had been made and the mission was on!

During the next two years I totally immersed myself in the world of the Mayan Mentalistas, an indigenous people of South America whose ancestors had undergone very early conversion to Christianity by the conquistadors. They went on to develop a culture whose science was star-based. The Mayan skull is an important centerpiece of their cosmology, whose oral traditions tell us that the skull originated on a planet, in our solar system, that was later destroyed. Some of the inhabitants of that planet ended up on Earth, on islands off the Yucatan. These were the islands of Atlantis, which were also eventually destroyed. The crystal skulls, however, had been transported ashore, into the Yucatan. All of these events predated the existence of the Mayans.

Some of the Atlantean structures are still extant in the Yucatan jungle but are incorrectly identified as being remnants of the Olmec and Mayan cultures. Tradition says that the Atlanteans who survived the destruction of Atlantis gave the skulls and star maps to the Mentalistas and taught them about our planet and our galaxy, in addition to teaching them how to survey land, utilize geometry, and navigate the seas. They also gave them tools and instruments for calculations.

The Mayans of today have a different reality, however, because in order to survive they have had to adapt to harsh circumstances imposed on them. This includes the trafficking of relics and contraband art, not only from their own culture, but from Europe and South America as well.

In the early 1900s President Diaz ordered his troops to stop at nothing to obtain the Mayan skull. When he succeeded, he kept the skull as private booty for many years and employed dark sorcerers to engage in psychic warfare against the Mayans who wanted the skull back and the Mentalistas who were warriors of the light. Diaz used the Mayan skull and his dark forces for nefarious purposes, including the attainment of information about his enemies. Eventually the Mayans were successful in launching a raid on the presidential palace and re-capturing the crystal skull.

While all this was going on, I was traveling back and forth from the jungles of the Yucatan to Mexico City and California. Unbeknownst to me, Francesco was making deals with South American Nazis and corrupt Mexican American businessmen who wanted to purchase the skull. Francesco was the Mayan who had been mandated to be the go-between for these gringos and those who controlled the relics. This was a very dangerous job, made even more so when Francesco lost the trust of the gringos and became their hostage. Under interrogation he was forced to reveal to his oppressors that the skulls were being held and protected by the Mayan Mentalistas.

This verification of the existence of the ancient crystal skulls buzzed through the Nazi network that was holding him prisoner! Lusting after the ultimate prize, they lobbied every soldier of fortune, collector, robber, and corrupt Mexican American businessman to converge on Mexico with the Mayan Mentalistas. The coveted crystal skull was in the center of their bull's eye.

Because Francesco had done a psychic reading on me, he knew that it was my destiny to be an integral part of this, and he revealed myriad previously undisclosed details to me at this time: He and his daughter were the last of the lineage of the Mayan Mentalistas who had been appointed caretakers of the skull. They, in turn, were due to pass it to Nick Nocerino, the Mentalista who would carry on the tradition of being its steward and guardian in the United States, for it was only in the United States that a study of the skull—utilizing modern science and technology—could be performed. It was here that the skull could be "opened" for communication and be utilized for the betterment of humanity as well as to usher in a new era of science.

However, given all of this, and despite the fact that it had been pre-ordained that I was to be a key player in this unfolding, I had yet to prove my worth and commitment. The next year would prove to be my rite of passage. During this time I would become, among other things, a smuggler. However, before getting more deeply involved, I needed to be absolutely certain that Francesco was legitimate. After all, I was in a foreign country that had become a multidimensional trick box. If the skull stayed in the cloistered world of the Mayan Mentalistas it would never fulfill its destiny. It would be my responsibility to be the guardian that would get it into North America. And I was the only one who could gather the right people together to do so.

Part of my preparation involved an excursion into the underworld, deep inside the barrios of Mexico City, a labyrinth that few gringos and outsiders ever see, and fewer still live to talk about. The men who frequent these barrios are men who peddle stolen artifacts, artwork, sacred relics, and artifacts from all over the world.

On the appointed day, I met Francesco at the appointed place at the appointed hour. Together he and I entered a building that was heavily guarded and filled with purveyors of the illicit trade. This was the place where antiquities and souls were bought and sold and transferred out to further networks of museums, shops, galleries—to connoisseurs and black market collectors.

In one of the rooms, sitting on a table was a crystal skull, stone masks, and figurines. Francesco picked up the skull and carried it into a back room, one without windows, lit by a single light. He did a blessing and then turned off the light. As he held the skull it suddenly began to emanate a rose-hued glow that had a neon purple aura. This glow became so strong that it comfortably lit the small room. Francesco laid down the skull and then soon returned carrying a jade mask. As he held it, light began to emanate from it as well. He was demonstrating the authenticity of the ancient artifacts and how the energy that they contained could be released by the Mentalista.

He passed each article to me so that I could experience the same effect. Francesco then mentally turned off both objects and, as he did so, the light left them. Now I was no longer operating on assumptions. What I had witnessed had served as proof positive of the validity of Francesco and the ancient crystal skull. We emerged from the small room, at which point Francesco placed the skull in a protective box and sealed it. I called Nick and told him that the skull and Francesco had both checked out as being genuine, which was his cue to board a plane and meet me in Mexico so that he and I could bring the skull back to the United States together as planned.

Unbeknownst to us, however, Francesco and I had been tailed by the Nazis, which we found out when we picked up Nick at the airport. What ensued was a wild car chase back to our hotel. Once safely inside, Francesco decided that because we were under such tight surveillance it would be best for us to leave for Oaxaca to shake the entourage that was following us.

However, they boarded the same plane we did! This convinced us that the time was not right for a hand-off of the Mayan skull, and because of this Nick returned to the United States alone. It would be several months before Nick could return and Francesco would have the unchecked ability to bring the Mayan crystal skull to our hotel. He never disclosed what he had to go through to do this, but accomplish it he did. Finally we were together again—brothers united in our destiny with the Mayan skull! Together we entered into a ceremony of prayer and communication with the skull.

As we meditated on it and peered into it together, the three of us witnessed the following: First, it divided itself into two skulls and then re-emerged back into one even larger than before. We were shown some scenes of Earth's history in accelerated time, in detail, and with great clarity.

Between the first and the second ice age, also known as eons or worlds, there was little evidence of civilization; we saw mostly land-scapes and a smaller Earth with some water but not oceans as we have now. Between the second and third eon the population of the planet was sparse, but there were some huge monolithic structures in the area we know now as Eurasia and northern India. Images of faces were presented, and we understood that the skull was present on Earth at this time and that these scenes were recorded by those whose faces we were seeing. Spacecraft were present. There were scenes of Earth that were so large we could see entire hemispheres.

When the scenes advanced to those of the third and the fourth eons we saw populated cities, some of which were colossal. The construction was enormous in stature as were the people—some of whom were giants. There were equally large aircraft of three main types: one was comprised of a large cylinder with outriggers that revolved; the second was a dark nonreflecting delta triangle; and the third was a similarly dull black, delta-shaped pentagon.

We saw populated cities, some monolithic and made with advanced materials and construction. The areas that we know as India and Tibet were thriving with commerce and interplanetary traffic. There was a lot of building taking place on the northwest side of the Indian continent, on a landmass that currently doesn't exist. The mountainous areas of the Himalayas as well as the Pyrenees in Europe weren't as high as they are now and weren't covered in ice but enjoyed a temperate climate.

In what we know today as Egypt pyramids were being constructed; they pre-date what remains today. On the South American continent massive construction was under way in the area known as the Andes. The majority of commerce taking place was via aircraft going back and forth on and off the planet, rather than terrestrial commerce. Later in this same eon, six extraordinarily large aircraft hovered above the mountainous region of the Andes and demolished the area as we looked on. Enemies of our planet in black delta and pentagon-shaped aircraft, miles in circumference, were using power beams to decimate the mountains. A few moments later, along the Pacific coastline of South America, a shelf dropped off and the Andes Mountains arose. Simultaneously, in the more populated India, the northwest side of that landmass suddenly submerged into the Arabian Sea.

The scenes then progressed into an ice age; during this time our planet expanded in size. The enemies in the aircraft continued to attack and decimate portions of Earth. Following this was a scene that was not of our planet but of a larger planet in our solar system where the same decimation was taking place, apparently by these same enemies.

At this point a dust cloud covered Earth as we entered into a new ice age. We were allowed to see our solar system and beyond. What we saw was the horizontal plane of a binary star system wherein we could view our sun as well as another sun far, far away. Then our vision became more concentrated as we focused again on Earth. We jumped forward to the end of the ice age and into the fourth world.

An expanded Earth was being revealed as the northern ice cap receded and a deluge of rain fell into what were now large oceans. The interplanetary traffic coming to and from Earth had been re-established and commerce was taking place. There were no terrestrial roadways or vehicles; instead everything was space-oriented. Landmasses from the prior scene were no longer extant, and huge islands the size of Australia had vanished. Our planet was thriving, humans were populating, agriculture was starting to thrive, and construction was under way. A power system was operational in that many buildings on Earth at this time contained artificial light.

Then we moved forward in time. In South America, Asia, Mexico, and Egypt the pyramids, as we know them today, were being built. We saw the Giza Pyramid, where Nick had acquired the crystal that he had given me. The pyramid was intact with porticos and a moat. (Nick later told us that the vision in the skull was the same one that he had intuitively glimpsed when he had been in Egypt during the war.) We also saw that evil was being planted on Earth at this time, which was the era of the pre-Olmecs when the crystal skulls had been moved from sunken Atlantis.

Then we came into what we call the modern era, which began approximately eight thousand years ago. At this point we saw humans begin to be dominant on Earth, with the help of "good angels." But what came next was another cycle of off-planet interdimensional war and terrestrial changes. As we viewed this time in "our" cycle we began to be impacted emotionally by what we were viewing. As the scenes faded from view we all felt incredibly exhausted by the immensity of information that had been downloaded to us.

We took a little while to process everything we had seen, and then we began to develop a plan to get the skull from Mexico to the United States, which Nick and I were able to pull off successfully. Safe now in the United States, Nick and I had only a short period of time in which to study the skull without interference. Please see chapter 8 for the incredible results of the testing that was done on this skull.

Notes

CHAPTER ONE. WHAT IS QUARTZ CRYSTAL?

1. www.technovelgy.com/ct/Science-Fiction-News.asp?NewsNum=458. Accessed Nov. 2011.
2. Wade, *Textbook of Precious Stones*, 56.
3. Personal communication with Wesley BlackElk and Terry Roses.
4. Steiner, *Cosmic Memory*.

CHAPTER TWO. THE HISTORY OF QUARTZ

1. www.alchemyandenergy.com/energetic feng shui space clearing/schumann resonance. Accessed Nov. 2011.
2. www.unesco.org/ext/field/beijing/whc/pkm-site.htm. Accessed Nov. 2011.
3. Ibid.
4. Ibid
5. Balibar, *The Science of Crystals*, 9.
6. www.crystalinks.com/mexicocrystals.html. Accessed Nov. 2011.
7. Dorland, *Holy Ice*, 58.
8. http://real-psychic-powers.com/delphic-oracle.html. Accessed Nov. 2011.
9. Pliny, *The Natural History of Pliny*, 394.
10. Rodriquez, *The Collected works of St. Theresa of Avila*.
11. Kunz, *The Curious Lore of Precious Stones*, 182.
12. Balibar, *The Science of Crystals*, 12.
13. Ibid.

14. Ibid., 20.

15. DeSalvo, *The Seeress of Prevorst.*

CHAPTER THREE.
PSYCHIC STUDIES OF QUARTZ CRYSTAL

1. Fowler, *The Andreasson Affair—Phase Two; The Watchers; The Watchers II; The Andreasson Legacy.*

CHAPTER FOUR.
QUARTZ CRYSTALS IN HEALING

1. DeSalvo, *Andrew Jackson Davis,* 10.

2. Ibid., 143.

CHAPTER FIVE.
THE ANCIENT CRYSTAL SKULLS

1. www.dreamscape.com/morgana/desecrat.htm. Accessed Nov. 2011.

2. Dorland, *Holy Ice,* 17–20.

3. Garvin, *The Crystal Skull,* 13–14.

4. www.crystalskulls.com/mitchell-hedges-crystal-skull.html. Accessed Nov. 2011.

5. Dorland, *Holy Ice,* 21–22.

6. Personal communication.

7. www.gizapyramid.com. Accessed Nov. 2011.

8. DeSalvo, *Decoding the Pyramids,* 120–25.

CHAPTER SIX.
ANCIENT HIMALAYAN
CRYSTAL SKULLS AND DROPA DISCS

1. Bowen, *Mysteries of the Crystal Skulls Revealed.*

2. Personal communication with Elizabeth HeartStar Keller.

3. Personal communication with Lynn Johnson.

CHAPTER SEVEN.
SCIENTIFIC STUDIES ON MY CRYSTAL SKULLS

1. Personal communication with Helene Olsen.
2. Personal communication with Ann Hall.

CHAPTER EIGHT.
OTHER RESEARCH AND RESULTS OF SCIENTIFIC TESTS
ON ALLEGED ANCIENT CRYSTAL SKULLS

1. Sax, et al., "The Origins of Two Purportedly Pre-Columbian Mexican Crystal Skulls," 2751–2760.
2. www.archaeology.org/online/features/mitchell_hedges/microscope.html. Accessed Nov. 2011.

CHAPTER NINE. SCRYING WITH CRYSTALS

1. DeSalvo, *Lost Art of Enochian Magic,* chapter 5.
2. Personal communication with Ukrainian scientist.

CHAPTER TWELVE. CRYSTALS IN ATLANTIS

1. Joseph, *Ark of the Cevenant.*
2. www.crystalinks.com/cayceatlantis.html. Accessed Nov. 2011.
3. DeSalvo, *Decoding the Pyramids.*

CHAPTER THIRTEEN. CRYSTALS IN ALIEN IMPLANTS

1. Ezekiel, chapter 1.
2. Personal communication with Becky Andreasson.
3. www.bibliotecapleyades.net/vida_alien/alien_andreasson.htm. Accessed Nov. 2011.
4. Fowler, *The Andreasson Affair—Phase Two; The Watchers; The Watchers II; The Andreasson Legacy.*
5. Personal communication with Becky Andreasson.
6. Ibid.
7. Ibid.

Bibliography

Balibar, Francoise. *The Science of Crystals.* New York: McGraw-Hill, 1993.

Bowen, Sandra. *Mysteries of the Crystal Skulls Revealed.* Pinole, Calif.: J & S Aquarian Networking, 1987.

Bryant, Alice, and Phyllis Galde. *The Message of the Crystal Skull.* St. Paul, Minn.: Llewellyn Publications, 1989.

DeSalvo, John. *Andrew Jackson Davis, The First American Prophet and Clairvoyant.* LuLu.com, 2005.

———. *Decoding the Pyramids.* New York: Barnes and Noble, 2008.

———. *The Seeress of Prevorst: Her Secret Language and Prophecies from the Spirit World.* Rochester, Vt.: Inner Traditions, 2008.

———. *The Lost Art of Enochian Magic.* Rochester, Vt.: Inner Traditions, 2010.

———. *Decoding the Enochian Secrets.* Rochester, Vt.: Inner Traditions, 2011.

Dorland, Frank. *Holy Ice.* St. Paul, Minn.: Galde Press, Inc., 1992.

Fowler, Raymond E. *The Andreasson Affair.* Englewood Cliffs, N.J.: Prentice-Hall, Inc., 1979.

———. *The Andreasson Affair—Phase Two.* Englewood Cliffs, N.J.: Prentice-Hall, Inc., 1982.

———. *The Watchers.* New York: Bantam Books, 1990.

———. *The Watchers II.* Newberg, Ore.: Wild Flower Press, 1995.

———. *The Andreasson Legacy.* New York: Marlowe and Company, 1997.

Galde, Phyllis. *Crystal Healing; The Next Step.* St. Paul, Minn.: Llewellyn Publications, 1988.

Garvin, Richard. *The Crystal Skull.* New York: Doubleday & Co., Inc. 1973.

Joseph, Frank. "The Crystal Skull: Ancient Artifact or Modern Fake?" *Ancient American* 5 (31) (2000, February): 4–9.

Joseph, Frank, and Laura Beaudoin. *Opening the Ark of the Covenant.* Franklin Lakes, N.J.: New Page Books, 2007.

Kunz, George Frederick. *The Curious Lore of Precious Stones.* Philadelphia, Pa.: Lippincott, 1913.

Leaf, Horace. *The Psychology and Development of Mediumship.* London: Rider & Co., 1926.

Moody, Raymond A. *Scrying: The Art of Female Divination.* Marietta, Ga.: R. Bemis Publishing Ltd., 1995.

Morrill, Sibley S. *The Mystery of Crystal Gazing: How an Ancient Mayan Skull May Be the Key.* San Francisco: Cadleon Publishing Co., 1969.

Morton, Chris, and Ceri Louise Thomas. *The Mystery of the Crystal Skulls.* Rochester, Vt.: Bear & Company, 1998.

Pliny. *The Natural History of Pliny,* volume 6. London: Bohn, 1857.

Rodriquez, Otilio. *The Collected Works of St. Theresa of Avila.* Washington, D.C.: ASICS Publishers, 1976.

Sax, Margaret. "The Identification of Carving Techniques on Chinese Jade." *Journal of Archaeological Science* 31 (2004): 1413–28.

———. "Methods of Engraving Mesopotamian Cylinder Seals: Experimental Confirmation." *Journal of Archaeological Science* 35 (2008): 2751–60.

Sax, Margaret, et al. "The Origins of Two Purportedly Pre-Columbian Mexican Crystal Skulls." *Journal of Archaeological Science* 35 (2008): 2751–60.

Steiner, Rudolf. *Cosmic Memory.* New York: Harper and Row, 1981.

van Etten, Jaap. *Crystal Skulls: Interacting with a Phenomenon.* Flagstaff, Ariz.: Light Technology Publishing, 2007.

Wade, Frank B. *A Textbook of Precious Stones.* New York: G. P. Putnam and Sons, 1918.

About the Author

John DeSalvo, Ph.D., is director of the Great Pyramid of Giza Research Association. His purpose in starting this association was to make available to the public general information and new research on the Great Pyramid.

A former college professor and administrator, his B.S. degree is in physics, and his M.A. and Ph.D. degrees are in biophysics. He has taught the following subjects on the college level: human anatomy and physiology, biochemistry, general biology, human gross anatomy, and neurophysiology. His college administrative experience includes positions as cultural affairs director, basic science department head, and dean of student affairs.

In 1979, DeSalvo coauthored the book *Human Anatomy—A Study Guide* (currently out of print) with Dr. Stanley Stolpe, former head of the Anatomy Department at the University of Illinois. His publications in scientific journals include research on the infrared system of rattlesnakes ("Spatial Properties of Primary Infrared Neurons in Crotalidae"). He was also a recipient of research grants and fellowships from the National Science Foundation, the United States Department of Public Health and Human Services, and the National Institutes of Health. For more than thirty years John DeSalvo was one of the scientists involved in studying the Shroud of Turin.

John DeSalvo with his life-size crystal skull, previously
owned by a well-known Argentinian anthropologist.
Photograph © John DeSalvo.

Currently he is executive vice president of ASSIST (Association
of Scientists and Scholars International for the Shroud of Turin),
which is the largest and oldest research association in the world currently studying the Shroud of Turin. He was also a research consultant to the original STURP (Shroud of Turin Research Project) team
and was the contributing science editor for the book *SINDON: A*
Layman's Guide to the Shroud of Turin (published in 1982, currently
out of print). His shroud research involved the image formation process of the man on the shroud and studies using three-dimensional
reconstruction, spectroscopic, and ultraviolet analysis. He has lec-

tured nation wide on the shroud, and in 1980 the International Platform Association designated him as one of the top thirty speakers in the nation.

He published *The Complete Pyramid Sourcebook* in 2003 and *Andrew Jackson Davis: The First American Prophet and Clairvoyant* in 2005. His book *Decoding the Pyramids* was published by Barnes and Noble in May 2008. In October 2008, his book *The Seeress of Prevorst: Her Secret Language and Prophecies from the Spirit World* was published by Inner Traditions. His book *Dead Sea Scrolls* was published by Barnes and Noble in July 2009.

His first book on magic, *The Lost Art of Enochian Magic,* was published by Destiny Books in 2010 and features a CD of DeSalvo pronouncing the Enochian Calls. His most recent book, which was also published by Destiny Books in 2011, is *Decoding the Enochian Secrets.*

DeSalvo family logo

Index